WATERSHED MANAGEMENT
EFFECTIVE TOOL FOR SUSTAINABLE LIVELIHOOD

ABOUT COUNCIL OF ANALYTICAL TRIBAL STUDIES (COATS) KORAPUT, ODISHA

COATS is a premier Research-cum-Academic Institute in the field of Tribal Studies. It is affiliated to Berhampur University, Odisha. COATS is a Registered Body under Societies Registration Act of 1860 bearing Registration No. 712/82 of 1991-92. It is situated in Koraput town in the district of Koraput, Odisha which is the heart of central tribal belt of the country.

COATS mainly aims at acquainting and educating the students, scholars and development workers about the tribal life, culture and development programmes. Presently, it imparts M.A. and M.Phil course in 'Tribal Studies' and its academic staff guide research scholars who are doing research leading to M.Phil and Ph.D. degrees in tribal affairs. The institute also undertakes District Planning and other evaluation studies entrusted to it from time to time both Central and State Governments. It organizes seminars, workshops and training programme from time to time.

About the Author

Anup Kumar Mohanty born in Koraput district of Odisha in the year 1967, is presently working as a senior faculty in Economics in Semiliguda College under Berhampur University. He has long years of teaching and research experience to his credit. He has completed his post-graduation studies in Analytical and Applied Economics from Utkal University. He has done his M.Phil in Tribal Studies from Council of Analytical Tribal Studies (COATS) under Berhampur University. He has completed his Ph.D. in Economics from Berhampur University in Natural Resource Management in the year 2011. He is also an Associate of Indian Institute of Advanced Studies (IIAS), Shimla. He is a honorary faculty of Council of Analytical Tribal Studies (COATS) and supervising two M.Phil and one Ph.D. scholar under this Institute. He has attended and presented papers in many National and International Seminars.

WATERSHED MANAGEMENT EFFECTIVE TOOL FOR SUSTAINABLE LIVELIHOOD

Anup Kumar Mohanty

Published for

Council of Analytical Tribal Studies (COATS)
Koraput

By

CONCEPT PUBLISHING COMPANY PVT. LTD.
NEW DELHI-110059

ISBN-13 : 978-93-5125-279-5

First Published 2017

Published and Printed by

Concept Since 1974

Concept Publishing Company Pvt. Ltd.
Regd. Office :
A/15-16, Commercial Block, Mohan Garden
New Delhi-110 059 (INDIA)
Phones : 011-25351460, 011-25351794, *Fax* : 091-11-25357109
E-mail : publishing@conceptpub.com
Website : www.conceptpub.com

Cataloging in Publication Data--Courtesy: D.K. Agencies (P) Ltd. <docinfo@dkagencies.com>

Mohanty, Anup Kumar, 1967- **author.**
Watershed management: effective tool for sustainable livelihood / Anup Kumar Mohanty.
pages cm
Includes bibliographical references and index.
ISBN 9789351252795

1. Watershed management--Government policy--India--Koraput (District) 2. Sustainable agriculture--India--Koraput (District) 3. Rural development--India--Koraput (District) 4. Tribes--India--Koraput (District) I. Council of Analytical Tribal Studies (India) II. Title.

HD1698.I42K67 2017 DDC 333.9100954133 23

FOREWORD

I have immense pleasure in going through the book by Dr. Anup Kumar Mohanty entitled, "Watershed Management: Effective Tool for Sustainable Livelihood". It is the outcome of his doctoral research undertaken under my supervision. It is the work of the scholar in Koraput district for making an assessment of the impact of the watershed development projects on the rainfed areas of the districts.

The present study is primarily an empirical work of the scholar in the interior pockets of Koraput district on the watershed projects undertaken by the Government and Non-Governmental Organizations. The author has selected a sample of 300 households from 20 watershed projects from 5 sample blocks of the district. He has made an in-depth analysis of the completed projects in Koraput district to find out its impact on social, economic and political life of the stakeholders of the area through five objectives.

The author after carefully examining the empirical data collected from the stakeholders found that after the functioning of the watershed projects in the rainfed areas of the district, the availability of irrigation facility has improved which led to higher productivity and diversification of crops in those areas. Due to the watershed projects the livestock population of the area has also increased due to the availability of fodder in the area.

The study reveals that the income of the sample households has increased substantially. There has been also an increase in the water table in the watershed areas. The percentage of people Below Poverty Line (BPL) of the study area has gone down drastically due to the implementation of the project.

The author has substantiated through empirical data, how there has been increase in the productivity of various crops and the diversification of crops from cereal to cash crops. The study has also revealed that the farmers mostly tribal (83%) are able to get bank finance for cultivation and other purposes through the Self-Help Groups (SHGs). Various activities are undertaken through the SHGs for the cooperative development of the entire village.

The author has also suggested a few practical suggestions to make the watershed programmes to perform better in a backward district like Koraput. He has emphasized on the role of NGOs for improving the organization of the watershed project.

The book will be a valuable guide to the research scholars, agriculture experts and the policy makers.

Date: 17-10-2016
Koraput (Odisha)

P.C. Mohapatro
Director, COATS

PREFACE

Koraput district of Odisha is known for the natural beauties and high concentration tribal population in the region. About half of its population is tribal, the tribes predominantly found in the district are the Khond, Paraja, Gadaba, Soura and Gond. This area is covered under tribal sub-plan area of the Central Government and many special programmes are being run to address the backwardness of the tribals of the district. The main occupation of the tribal people is agriculture which is supplemented by collection of minor forest produce. The shifting cultivation by the indigenous people is also one of the unique features of these tribes. The farm size is very small due to fragmentation and agriculture is mostly rainfed. The tribal people are educationally and economically very backward and they follow the traditional methods of cultivation which result in low crop productivity. Most part of Koraput district are totally dependent on the rainwater. Hence, they mostly cultivate *kharif* crops but are unable to use the rainwater properly due to poor knowledge about the soil and water conservation practices.

With a view to increase the crop productivity from dryland farming and to prevent the deterioration of natural resources watershed development programmes with modern components were implemented in the State and Koraput district since early 1990s. A huge amount of money is being spend by various implementing agencies for a sustainable livelihood for the rainfed farmers.

Hence, a research was planned to find out the effectiveness of the programme which is meant for the holistic development of the rainfed areas in the country. The present study was conducted in 20 watershed villages in five blocks of Koraput district and a sample size of 300 households were selected for the purpose of evaluation of the projects. The major parameters included in the evaluation process are social, economic and environmental aspects of the stakeholders of the area. The findings of this study will help the policy-makers, researchers and social workers to plan their strategies for promoting the use of soil and water conservation practices in the tribal area.

I express my deep sense of gratitude to Prof. Prafulla Chandra Mohapatra, Director, Council of Analytical Tribal Studies (COATS),

Koraput and Prof. Jagabandhu Samal, Professor Tribal Studies COATS, Koraput for their guidance and encouragement for publication of the book.

I am thankful to Sri Sanjay Kumar Nanda, Deputy Director, District Planning and Monitoring Unit (DPMU), Koraput, Sri Pranab Ranjan Choudhury, Freelance Consultant, Sri Dayanidhi Bagh, Asst. Director, Soil Conservation, Koraput for their cooperation in providing the official information and valuable inputs into the watershed programmes undertaken in the district.

I am grateful to staff of DRDA, Koraput and Project Director, Watershed Koraput, Central Soil and Water Conservation and Research Institute (CSWCRTI), Sunabeda and Water Technology Centre for Eastern Region (WTCER), Bhubaneswar for providing useful inputs in the research work. I am also equally thankful to the entire staff of COATS for the cooperation given to me in completion of research work.

Anup Kumar Mohanty

ACKNOWLEDGEMENTS

It is my proud privilege to express my heartfelt gratitude, humble regards and everlasting obligation to my revered guide Dr. Prafulla Chandra Mohapatra, Director, Council of Analytical Tribal Studies (COATS), Koraput who graciously accepted the burden of supervision of the study in spite of his several preoccupations. I have the honour and privilege to express my deep sense of respect and sincere gratitude to Dr. Jagabandhu Samal, Professor of Tribal Studies, COATS, Koraput for his advises and supervision of my work at various stages and constant encouragement which inspired me to complete the work in a time bound manner.

I am very much thankful to my Principal Sri Rabi Narayan Sutar and the staff of Semiliguda College, Semiliguda for their cooperation and support in completing the project in time.

I am equally thankful to Sri Sanjay Kumar Nanda, Deputy Director, District Planning and Monitoring Unit, Koraput, Sri Dayanidhi Bag, Assistant Director, Soil Conservation, Koraput, Sri Pranab Ranjan Choudhury, Consultant, JBIC Projects, Sri Surendra Karan, Director, Centre for Development and Research and Training (CDRT), Koraput, Dr. Abhilash Nayak, Regional Director, IGNOU, Bhubaneswar and Sri Prafulla Kumar Sethi, Branch Manager, Andhra Bank, Semiliguda in the fieldwork and the help they have provided at various stages of the work.

I am grateful to the staff of District Rural Development Agency (DRDA), Koraput and Project Director Watershed, Koraput, Central Soil and Water Conservation Research and Training Institute (CSWCRTI), Sunabeda, Water Technology Centre for Eastern Region (WTCER), Bhubaneswar for providing me the required information and statistics about the watershed projects in Koraput district and Odisha.

I am thankful to the Programme Implementing Agency (PIA), Watershed Development Team Members, Watershed Committee members for their support in collection of data and other information regarding the watershed projects.

I am thankful to the entire staff of Council of Analytical Tribal Studies (COATS) for their cooperation in completing my project in time. I am also thankful to Mr. Laxminarayan Hota, Mr. Siba Prasad Patnaik,

Mr. B. Jagdish Kumar, Mr. Mukesh Nayak and Mr. Akshaya Limal for their cooperation in collection of data and preparation of the project report in time.

Last but not the least, I am thankful to my wife Ambuja Mohanty, my children Anisha and Anushri and my parents, brothers and sister for their sacrifice and constant encouragement throughout my study.

Anup Kumar Mohanty

CONTENTS

LIST OF TABLES

LIST OF FIGURES

LIST OF MAPS

LIST OF PHOTOGRAPHS

ABBREVIATIONS

ACA	Additional Central Assistance
BCM	Billion Cubic Metre
BPL	Below Poverty Line
BRGF	Backward Region Grant Fund
CD	Community Development
COWDEP	Comprehensive Watershed Development Programme
CPR	Common Property Resources
CSWCRTI	Central Soil and Water Conservation Research and Training Institute
DDP	Desert Development Programme
DFID	Department for International Development
DoLR	Department of Land Resources
DPAP	Desert Prone Area Programme
DPR	Detailed Project Report
DRDA	District Rural Development Agency
DWDU	District Water Development Unit
EAS	Employment Assurance Scheme
EEC	European Economic Council
EPA	Entry Point Activities
FAO	Food and Agricultural Organisation
GoI	Government of India
GoO	Government of Odisha
GP	Gram Panchayat
HYV	High Yielding Varieties
ICAR	Indian Council for Agricultural Research
ICRISAT	International Crop Research Institute for Semi-Arid Tropics
IDCWDP	Indo-Danish Comprehensive Watershed Development Programme
IFAD	International Fund for Agricultural Development
IGNRM	Integrated Genetic Natural Resource Management
INRM	Integrated Natural Resource Management
IWMP	Integrated Watershed Management Programme

JFMC	Joint Forest Management Committee
KBK	Koraput-Bolangir-Kalahandi
MGNREGS	Mahatma Gandhi National Rural Employment Guarantee Scheme
MoA	Ministry of Agriculture
MoEF	Ministry of Environment and Forest
MoRD	Ministry of Rural Development
NARS	National Agricultural Research Centre
NFFWP	National Food for Work Programme
NGO	Non-Governmental Organisation
NRAA	National Rainfed Area Authority
NRSA	National Remote Sensing Agency
NWDP	National Wasteland Development Programme
ORLP	Odisha Rural Livelihood Programme
OTELP	Odisha Tribal Empowerment and Livelihood Project
PIA	Project Implementing Agency
PRA	Participatory Rural Appraisal
RKVY	Rashtriya Krishi Vikas Yojana
RLTAP	Revised Long-Term Action Plan
RVP	River Valley Projects
SAT	Semi-Arid Tropics
SC	Scheduled Caste
SCA	Special Central Assistance
SGSY	Swarna Jayanti Swarojagar Yojana
SHG	Self-Help Group
SLNA	State Level Nodal Agency
ST	Scheduled Tribe
UG	User Group
UNDP	United Nations Development Programme
WA	Watershed Association
WC	Watershed Committee
WDP	Watershed Development Project
WDPSCA	Watershed Development Projects in Shifting Cultivation Areas
WHS	Water Harvesting Structure
WORLP	Western Odisha Livelihood Project
ZP	Zilla Parishad

1

INTRODUCTION

Importance of the Study

Rainfed system dominates world food production, but water investments in rainfed agriculture have been neglected over the past 50 years. Upgrading rainfed agriculture promises large social, economic and environmental paybacks, particularly in poverty reduction and economic development. Rainfed farming covers most of the world's croplands (80%) and produces most of the world's cereal grains (more than 60%), generating livelihoods in rural areas and producing food for cities. Estimate suggests that about 25 per cent of the increased water requirement needed to attain the 2015 hunger reduction target of the Millennium Development Goal can be contributed from irrigation. The remaining 75 per cent will have to come from water investment in rainfed agriculture.

Low productivity in rainfed areas, aggravated by water scarcity, degraded and poorly managed land, poor infrastructure and lack of market facility marginalises agriculture and livelihoods of the people in rainfed areas. Globally, 80 per cent of the agriculture is rainfed; in South Asia it is about 60-65 per cent. About 66 per cent of total arable land (142 million ha) in India is rainfed and suffers acute moisture stress. Although green revolution helped South Asia particularly India to attain self-sufficiency in food production, it bypassed millions of poor living in rainfed areas. Water is a critical constraint in increasing agricultural productivity. It is estimated that by the year 2025 one-third of the population of the developing countries, including 50 per cent of the population of India and China, will be facing physical scarcity of water (Molden *et al.*, 2007).

Agriculture has been the major source of livelihood in the Indian economy. Notwithstanding, major diversifications in the structure of the economy over the last few years the dependence on agriculture continues unabated. Agriculture development is key to economic development in India. As majority of the population depend on primary sector for their livelihood it is simply not possible to ignore this sector. Lack of irrigation facility in two-third arable land is one of the important reasons for low productivity and non-implementation of green revolution in our country.

In India even after full exploitation of irrigation potential about 60 per cent of the arable land continue to depend on rainfed farming. Both surface and ground water resources are under considerable pressure and have depleted considerably. Falling ground water table due to excessive exploitation and low recharge have led to disastrous consequences. In most rainfed areas, water availability is not a problem but rainfall distribution and poor water management creates water scarcity for crops resulting in low rainwater use efficiency (40-45%) and low crop productivity.

It is important to note that green revolution initiated in mid 1960s was largely confined to irrigated areas which account for about 35 per cent of the total cultivated area. The rainfed area is almost double the irrigated area and contributes only 45 per cent of the total foodgrain production of our country. Rainfed agriculture is characterized by low levels of productivity and low input usage. Due to the dependence on rainfall, the productivity varies from year-to-year depending on the volume of rainfall of that particular year. These areas show wide variation and instability in yields. The gap between yield potentials and actual yields is very high as compared to the irrigated areas. The rainfed regions of eastern India have the potential to achieve higher yields. India's agriculture has entered a post-green revolution stage that requires new strategies to enhance agricultural growth and reduce rural poverty. A move to an intensive diversified productivity with strong forward and backward linkages is the next evolutionary step in the country's future agricultural development.

Intervention Strategy

The Government of India gives high priority for the holistic and sustainable development of rainfed areas based on watershed approach. The watershed development projects are designed to harmonize the use of water, soil and forest resources in such a manner that it conserves their resources while raising agricultural productivity. A watershed is defined as a topographically delineated geographical area in which the entire run-off tends to converge through the existing draining system to the common outlet of the area for subsequent disposal. The implementation of watershed management project is not the end by itself but is one of the many useful means of development. A watershed project is viewed as one of the instruments for bringing about various social, cultural, political and economic changes in favour of the disadvantaged groups in rural areas.

The Strategy

The watershed approach aims at a participatory process to improve the natural resource base and living standard of the people dependent on these resources. The watershed management approach includes an elaborate institutional mechanism to ensure people's participation consisting of formation of Watershed Association (WA) comprising of all adults residing within watershed project area, involving formation of Watershed Committee (WC), an executive body consisting of 10-12 nominated members by the WA from among the User Groups (UGs), Self-Help Groups (SHGs), Gram Panchayat (GP), Watershed Development Team (WDT), which implements the project with the technical guidance of Programme Implementing Agency (PIA)/ Watershed Development Team (WDT).

Watershed management involves harnessing rainfall for improvement of barren hill slopes, privately owned lands, commonly owned lands and water resources in rainfed areas with people's participation. It begins with two most important resources, i.e., water and land. Management of macro-watersheds for ecological regions such as reduction in siltation in reservoirs has been there in India since long in the form of river valley projects. However, management of micro-watersheds for ecological and livelihood reasons has been of recent origin (Farrington *et al.*, 1999).

Watershed development has emerged as a major strategy of rural development especially to address the concerns and problems of rainfed hinterlands, a major contributor to the food security but mostly left behind by the 'green revolution'. The importance of rainfed agriculture is slowly being recognized among policy-makers and special efforts are being suggested for rainfed area development and the watershed development approach is now being propagated as something that will provide a major impetus in this direction. Even though watershed development is being practised for the last three decades, of late its scope is being re-cast to bring together different sectors and agendas with the major objective of sustainable development of rainfed areas and the communities dependent on them. With this widening scope, the policy direction of the programme itself has undergone several changes initiated by C.H. Hanumantharao Committee recommendations in the early nineties and culminating in the recent common guidelines (A. Samuel *et al.*, 2008).

However, there is a paucity of reliable large-scale information/ studies on the long-term potential and impacts of watershed across the regions. Despite the growing importance of watershed projects as an approach to rural development and natural resource management, to date there has not been much research on the impact assessment of these projects. Research is needed to ensure that new projects benefit from the positive and negative experiences of their predecessors. Evaluation is difficult, however due to the social and technical complexity of the watershed projects.

Watershed development programmes are being implemented in this district under various Central and State sponsored programmes like Integrated Wasteland Development Programme (IWDP), National Watershed Development Programme for Rainfed Area (NWDPRA), River Valley Projects (RVP). Watershed programmes are also being taken up Special Central Assistance (SCA) under RLTAP programme for the KBK districts of Odisha. Recently, Odisha Livelihoods Programme called JEEBIKA has been launched in Koraput district out of the six districts selected in this State. The State Government has also been allowed to utilize the resources of Central Government under the Employment Assurance Scheme (EAS), and Additional Central Assistance (ACA) for the management of watershed projects. Till January 2009, a sum of ₹ 41.43 crore (DRDA, Koraput) have been spent for the watershed development projects under various schemes and the State Government is implementing new programmes through the Odisha Tribal Empowerment and Livelihood Programme (OTELP) and Jeebika programme which gives emphasis on the livelihood support for the rural poor. Many watershed projects have been/are being implemented in collaboration with the foreign aid. The Indo-Danish Comprehensive Watershed Development Programme (IDCWDP) is one such programme implemented in two blocks of this district. The Non-Governmental Organizations (NGOs) working in this district also implement the watershed development programmes in collaboration with the State Government and other of national and international donor agencies.

The objective of the study is to assess the impact of the programmes undertaken by various Government departments and Non-Governmental Organizations (NGOs) on the stakeholders of the area and its environment.

The various WDPs have been selected from among the projects implemented during the period 1997-98 to 2006-07. The broad objective is to assess the impact of the watershed programmes on the beneficiaries during and after the completion of the project.

The Study Area: A Profile

Koraput district where the study was conducted is one of the southern most districts of Odisha. It has higher concentration of tribal population and comes under the tribal sub-plan area. The major tribal communities found in this region are the Kondhs, Parajas, Bhotadas, Sauras, Gadabas and Durua, etc. Other important social groups are that of Scheduled Caste which includes various castes like the Dambo, Ganda, Ghasi, Chandala, Pana, Relli, etc. The percentage of ST population of this district is 49.62 per cent of total, SC population 13.04 per cent, literacy is 35.72 per cent, female literacy is 24.26 per cent and rural population is 83.19 per cent (2001, Census). The percentage of below poverty line population is 83.81 per cent. With more than 80 per cent of the population in this area living below the official poverty line, the socio-economic indicators in these areas are comparable to the worst in the world. Unlike rest of Odisha and India, the poverty incidence in these area show an increase in last two decade, the percentage of people living below $1/day have increased from 73 per cent in 1983 to 85 per cent in 2000 in Koraput district. The extreme backwardness of these areas has drawn attention of State and Central Government as well as international donor agencies and it has led to a plethora of development interventions, including watershed development and other natural resources projects.

The Koraput district of Odisha consists of hills of Eastern Ghats discontinuous range of mountains, river valleys of Indravati, Kolab, Nagavali as well as number of plateaus. The altitude ranges between 300-1500 mtrs above the mean sea level. Mean average annual rainfall is 1,521 mm. Agro-climatically the region lies in the Agro-Ecological zone which is known as "Eastern Ghat High Land Zone" of Odisha. Forest type ranges from Semi-evergreen forests to dry deciduous forests. This region has high bio-diversity, not only in the forests, but also in the varieties of cultivated species. As a matter of fact, this tract is the primary centre of origin of rice. The official net sown area on an average ranges around 25 per cent of the total area of the region and the total irrigated area is only one-third of the cultivated area as the undulating topography of the region restricts the expansion of the flow and lift irrigation. Paddy is the major crop of the region occupying about 50 per cent of the total cropped area and forms the staple diet of the tribal along with finger millet.

About 70 per cent of land in agriculture is rainfed, and irrigation is primarily through the Jhola systems or small diversion weirs. There is only one medium irrigation project, i.e. the Upper Kolab Irrigation Project providing irrigation to 45,000 hectares of land of the relatively plain area. Thus, the agricultural production is highly dependent on the rain and management of run-off water within the watersheds. Apart from the *jholas* and some medium land, agriculture including shifting cultivation (podu chàsa) is carried out on sloping land which given the soil type and high intensity rainfall are highly vulnerable to soil erosion and gully formation. Loss of vegetation on slopes and upstream areas also make the *jholas* and medium lands vulnerable to sand casting and crop being washed off in intense rains (Kundan Kumar *et al.*, 2006).

Watershed Development Strategy

Natural increase in population, immigration of outsiders, displacement through major development projects and reservation of land as forests have increased the pressure on land in the last sixty years. This has especially affected the higher hill slopes where shifting cultivation cycle has been reduced, leading to soil and vegetation degradation. With the high livelihood dependence on natural resources, subsistence agriculture, hilly and rugged topography, ongoing degradation of resources and high potential for natural resources based development, watershed development has emerged as an important development strategy in the region.

Koraput and its adjoining districts of the States of Andhra Pradesh and Chhattisgarh are situated in the Agro-climatic zone 12 are inhabitated mostly by tribal people. Land use practices of the tribal people like shifting cultivation, uncontrolled grazing, large-scale mining, faulty agriculture and overexploitation of forests have resulted in various forms of erosion in the area due to lack of vegetative cover. The erratic rainfall, undulating topography and unfavourable edaphic factors resulted in unpredictable production system with extreme cases of crop failure. The study area comes under Koraput-Bolangir- Kalahandi (KBK) region which is considered as one of the most backward regions of the country. The indicators of human development indices like literacy, per capita income, infant mortality rate, maternal mortality rate are alarming. About 84 per cent of the population of the area live below poverty line and most of them depend on agriculture and its allied activities for their living. About 34 per cent of the cultivable land area of the district is irrigated and the rest depends on the vagaries of monsoon for agricultural activities. To improve the condition of these downtrodden sections of the society, it is important to give emphasis on the boost in the agricultural productivity.

The objective of the study is to assess the impact of the programme undertaken by various government departments and Non-Governmental Organizations (NGOs) on the stakeholders and on the ecology of the study area. The various WDPs have been selected from among the projects implemented during the period 1997-98 to 2006-07. The broad objective is to assess the impact of watershed programmes on the beneficiaries during and after completion of the project.

Objectives

The main objectives of the study conducted were as follows:

1. To examine the extent of additional irrigation potential created through watershed projects.
2. To find out the growth in the agricultural productivity and crop diversification in the region.
3. To find out the extent of ecological changes due to watershed programmes.
4. To assess the impact of watershed programme on the livestock of the area.
5. To find out the socio-economic development of the rural people of this area.

Methodology

The Samples: To assess the impact of watershed programmes on the lives of tribal people of Koraput district five out of fourteen blocks have been selected purposively on the basis of irrigation potentialities of the blocks. Some of the highest and lowest irrigated blocks have been selected purposively to assess its impact. These blocks are — Pottangi, Semiliguda, Laxmipur, Borigumma, Boipariguda. From each block four watershed projects were selected on a random sampling basis and fifteen household from each watershed were randomly selected as sample. A total of 300 households have been taken as sample size (20 households from each watershed area) has been taken on simple random sampling basis.

Data Collection: The study is based on both primary as well as secondary sources of data collection. The primary data was collected from 300 respondents through a structured questionnaire prepared by the researcher for the purpose. From each watershed area 20 numbers of households were selected on the basis of simple random sampling. The survey was conducted in the year 2008-09. The format of the questionnaire was such that the information could be easily transformed on an individual basis. The survey was one-shot and repeated survey was not practicable. The household data were based purely on memory recall of the respondents with cross-checking from co-residents. The mode of data collection involves, (i) direct questioning of household head and other members; (ii) extracting data from the participant observations; and (iii) interviewing of the selected informants.

The secondary source of data collection was from various published information by Government and private agencies, research articles, books and journals and magazines and newspapers. Various electronic resources like the online journals, books, article and reference to websites of various departments and organizations have also been taken. It has been assumed that the data published by the above mentioned sources are authentic. For the purpose of analyzing the data, various statistical tools like simple arithmetic mean, percentage, ratio, probability, ANOVA, coefficient of variation and standard deviation have been used. The analysis of data has been represented through tables, charts, diagrams and graphs.

Limitations of the Study

Due to time and financial constraints sampling method have been used while drawing some conclusions instead of the census method of data collection which may have limitations of representation. Similarly, the scholar has relied on information and data available from various secondary sources like books, journal, research article, official and non-official reports, published and unpublished reports, information available on the internet. As the data is collected from the respondents by the investigator, the personal bias of the investigator at times distorts the facts. The accuracy of the impact of the project is dependent on the information provided by the respondents which may not always be correct as respondents may hide some of the facts due to some personal and other reasons and reporting from memory may not be hundred per cent correct. There may be some communication gap between the scholar and respondents as most of the households of the study area are tribal and illiterate. Despite all the above limitations as the case in every research the best effort has been made to see the sample taken from the study represents the universe in the best possible manner.

2

THE WATERSHED DEVELOPMENT
A Conceptual Analysis

Introduction

Rainfed agriculture in the India's Semi-Arid Tropics (SAT) is characterized by low productivity, degraded natural resources and widespread poverty. The people living in the semi-arid tropics depend mostly on agriculture and natural resources for their livelihood. Rainfed agriculture is diverse and risk prone due to the variability of the amount of rainfall during the monsoon season.

Rainfed Agriculture — A Macro-Analysis

When it comes to ensuring food security for all, two major water realities face humankind. Rainfed agriculture will continue to produce bulk of world's food and productivity is very low in rainfed agriculture, thus providing significant opportunities for producing more food with less fresh water. Rainfed agriculture is practiced in 80 per cent of the world's physical agricultural area and generates 62 per cent of the world's staple food (FAOSTAT, 2005). A new green revolution is the need of the hour in small-scale rainfed agriculture in arid, semi-arid and dry sub-humid regions of the world. This can be possible by investing in the untapped potential of upgrading rainfed agriculture through integrated water investments.

The importance of rainfed agriculture varies regionally but produces most foods for poor communities in developing countries. In sub-Saharan Africa more than 95 per cent of the farmed land is rainfed, while the corresponding figure for Latin America is almost 90 per cent, for South Asia it is about 60 per cent, for East Asia about 65 per cent and for near East and North Africa 75 per cent (FAOSTAT, 2005). Most countries in the world depend primarily on rainfed agriculture for their foodgrain.

Despite large strides made in improving productivity and environmental conditions in many developing countries, a great number of poor families in Africa and Asia still face poverty, hunger, food insecurity and malnutrition where rainfed agriculture is main agricultural activity. These problems are exasperated by adverse bio-physical growing conditions and poor socio-economic infrastructure in many areas in the Semi-Arid Tropics (SAT). The SAT is home to 38 per cent of the developing countries poor, 75 per cent of whom live in rural areas. Over 45 per cent of the world's hungry and more than 70 per cent of its malnourished children live in semi-arid tropics (S.P. Wani *et al.*, 2009).

The agricultural productivity has seen a rapid growth since the late 1950s due to new crop varieties, fertilizer use and expansion in irrigated agriculture. The world food production outstripped the population growth. However, there are regions of food insecurity. Of the 6.5 billion populations today, about 850 million people face food insecurity. About 60 per cent of them live in South Asia and sub-Saharan Africa. Food and crop demand is estimated to double in next 50 years. According to a comprehensive assessment, it is possible to produce food — but, it is probable that today's food production and environmental trends, if continued will lead to crises in many parts of the world (Molden, 2007).There is a close correlation between hunger, poverty and water: most hungry and poor people live in regions where water challenges pose a particular constraint to food production. The world's hotspots for hunger and poverty are concentrated in the arid, semi-arid and sub-humid regions of the world. There water is a key challenge for food production due to the extreme variability of rainfall, long dry season and recurrent droughts, floods and dry spells. These regions cover some 40 per cent of the world's land area and host roughly 40 per cent of the world's population. The water challenge in these rainfed areas is to enhance yields by improving water availability and water uptake capacity of crops.

Even with growing urbanization, globalization and better governance in Africa and Asia, hunger, poverty and vulnerability of livelihood to natural and other disasters will continue to be greatest threats in the rural SAT. These challenges are complicated by climatic variability, the risk of climate change, population growth and health pandemics (AIDS and Malaria), degrading natural resource base, poor infrastructure and changing pattern of demand and production (Ryan and Spencer, 2001). The majority of the poor in developing countries live in rural areas; their livelihood depends on agriculture. Overexploitation of natural resource base is pushing them into a downward spiral of poverty. The importance of rainfed source of food weighs disproportionately on women, given that 70 per cent of the world's poor are women (WHO, 2000). Agriculture plays a key role for economic development (World Bank, 2005) and poverty reduction (Irz and Roe, 2000) with evidence indicating that every 1 per cent increase in agricultural yields translates to a 0.6 to 1.2 per cent decrease in percentage of absolute poor (Thirtle *et al.*, 2002). As most of the semi-arid tropic poor are farmers and landless labourers, strategies for the reducing poverty, hunger and malnutrition should be driven primarily by the needs of the rural poor and should aim to build and diversify their livelihood sources. Substantial gains in land, water and labour productivity as well as better management of natural resources are essential to reverse the downward spiral of poverty and environment and environment degradation.

Rainfed Agriculture — The Indian Case

Low productivity in rainfed areas, aggravated by water scarcity, degraded and poorly managed land, poor infrastructure and lack of market, marginalizes agriculture and livelihoods. About 66 per cent of total arable land (142 million ha) in India is rainfed and suffers acute moisture stress. Although Green Revolution helped Asia particularly India, to attain self-sufficiency in food production, it by-passed millions of poor living in rainfed areas. Water is a critical constraint to increasing agricultural productivity. It is expected that by 2025, one-third of population in developing countries, including 50 per cent of the population of India and China will be facing physical scarcity of water. The recent Comprehensive Assessment of Water for food and water for life showed that challenges of food security with looming water scarcity cannot be met by irrigated agriculture alone, major gains have to come through upgrading rainfed agriculture (Molden *et al.*, 2007).

In India, even after exploitation of full irrigation potential, about 60 per cent of the arable area will continue to depend on rainfed farming. Both surface and groundwater resources are under considerable pressure and have depleted completely. Falling groundwater table, due to excessive exploitation and low recharge have led to disastrous consequences. The Central Groundwater Board of India has identified 100 critical districts in the country where excessive use of groundwater has led to serious economic and sustainability problems and 85 of these districts are situated in rainfed areas. Estimates of water availability *vis-à-vis* water requirement in 2050 indicate a yawning gap between demand and supply. Projections of water requirements show that in 2050, the country's utilizable water availability of 1,122 km^3/year will hardly be able to match the estimated requirement of 1,450 km^3/year (Gupta and Deshpande, 2004). The agriculture sector is the single largest user of water which accounts for more than 80 per cent of the total present demand. Estimates show that about 68 per cent of the total water requirement would be available for irrigation sector in 2050 (Sharma, 2002). It indicates an alarming situation in the years to come. In most rainfed areas, water availability is not a problem but rainfall distribution and poor management creates water scarcity for crops, resulting in low rainwater use efficiency (40-45%) and low crop production (Wani *et al.*, 2003). Rainwater stored in soil largely escape to atmosphere through unproductive evaporation and large water productivity gains could be achieved in rainfed areas by changing vapour flows productive evapotranspiration (green water) (Rockstorm *et al.*, 2007).

This is a matter of concern and requires developing appropriate strategies that ensure augmentation of water resources through all possible measures, including rainwater conservation and harvesting as well as efficient and economical use of water in rainfed areas. Development of watershed/catchments is one of the most trusted and eco-friendly approaches to manage rainwater and other natural resources, which has paid rich dividends in the rainfed areas and is capable of addressing many natural, social and environmental intricacies (Sarma, 1998). Management of natural resources at catchment/watershed scale produces multiple benefits in terms of increasing food productions, improving livelihoods, protecting the environment and addressing the gender and equity issues along with bio-diversity concerns. Watershed Development Programmes (WDPs) are therefore considered as a growth engine for the development of fragile and marginal rainfed areas (Wani *et al.*, 2008).

The most important feature of watershed development is *in-situ* conservation and harvesting rainwater for augmenting surface and ground resources in rainfed areas. Watershed development aims at optimum and prudent use of soil and water resources in sustainable and cost-effective mode. Augmentation of water resources is at the heart of WDPs (P.K. Joshi *et al.*, 2009). The catchment watershed development approach is a viable option for unlocking the potential of rainfed areas and doubling or quadrupling the productivity through augmenting water resources in the rainfed areas (Rockstorm, 2007). Watershed management is of strategic importance in bringing the second green revolution and achieving the goal of 4 per cent agricultural growth in the country. The Government of India has therefore accorded high priority to the holistic and sustainable development of rainfed areas through the integrated watershed development programmes (Wani *et al.*, 2008).

The concept of integrated and participatory watershed development and management has emerged as the cornerstone of rural development in the dry and semi-arid regions and other rainfed regions of the world and is a paradigm shift from earlier plot based approaches to soil and water conservation. The watershed approach enables planners to harmonize the use of soil, water and vegetation in a way that conserves these resources and maximize their productivity. The watershed is the appropriate hydrological unit for technical efforts to manage water and soil resources for production and conservation. But watershed management is complicated by the fact that watershed rarely correspond to human defined boundaries. The fundamental social problem of watershed development is that it often distributes benefits and costs unevenly, making it a likely source of disagreement and conflict. Mostly watershed projects distribute cost and benefits unevenly, with cost incurred disproportionately upstream, typically among the poor farmers, and benefits realized disproportionately downstream, where water use is concentrated and richer farmers own most of the land. The challenge is to internalize the costs and benefits in such a way that all the stakeholders are part of a win-win scenario (Sharma *et al.*, 2004).

Over the last couple of decades, the Government of India has addressed the challenges of watershed development and made major investments through an appropriate mix of technical innovation, participatory approaches. There is certainly evidence of positive impacts in terms of improved soil and water conservation and agricultural productivity in normal rainfall years in regions that have been ignored in the conventional green revolution based rural development (Samra, 1999). Countries in sub-Saharan Africa, South-East Asia and even China look towards India to learn from these experiences and adopt this natural resource based rural development model. However, overall gains from watershed development have not been equitably shared, either within the farming community or between different geographical settings.

The emphasis is on the augmentation of water resources by implementing small watershed projects. The majority of watershed development projects in the country are sponsored and implemented by the Government of India with the help of various state departments, Non-governmental organizations, self-help groups, etc. The Drought

Prone Area Programme (DPAP), the Desert Development Programme (DDP), the National Watershed Development Project for Rainfed Areas (NWDPRA), the Watershed Development in Shifting Cultivation Areas (WDSCA), the Integrated Watershed Development Project (IWDP) are a few of the important development programmes that plan, fund and implement watershed development projects. A total sum of US $7 billion has been invested in the country in various watershed development projects since inception (early 1980s) of WDPs until 2006. Several international organizations, including the Department for International Development (DFID), the Swiss Agency for Development and Cooperation (SDC), the World Bank and the International Fund for Agricultural Development (IFAD) also sponsor and implement watershed development projects but a significant proportion (about 70%) of the investments in WDPs is being made by the Government of India. Evidence shows that WDPs have yielded considerable benefits in terms of increasing agricultural productivity, groundwater recharge, reducing run-off and soil loss, increasing greenery, diversifying cropping systems, conserving bio-diversity, equity, sustainability and efficiency (Kerr *et al.*, 2000).

The watershed development approach in India has evolved over time, based on the knowledge gained from various programmes. It started with soil and water conservation programme and then laid emphasis on water harvesting and increasing crop productivity and recently focused on full livelihood improvement programmes. Although new approaches such as livelihood improvement and productivity enhancement are developed and proven their superiority, large number of watershed programmes has not graduated fully into livelihood support programmes till date and serves only as a soil and water conservation tool for the farmers.

In Asia and Africa, hundreds of millions of poor and marginal farmers rely on degraded land and water resources and struggle to cope with a diverse array of agro-climatic, production and market risks. It is estimated that the rate of land degradation in the rainfed area in India in the 1990s is basically on account of the soil erosion. At the same time, the region in particular and world in general does not have enough utilizable water needed to grow the food to adequately feed the future generations. The world is rapidly converting forest, wetland and other critical habitats into agricultural land to meet growing demands and diverting major rivers to produce food. The challenge of how to produce more and better food and maintain or improve critical ecosystem services without further undermining the environment is a major challenge.

The Watershed Management Concept

Definitions: Based on the conceptual premises adopted for the purpose, several agencies have suggested their own definitions of watershed management. Some of the widely acknowledged definitions are:

1. Watershed Management is the integrated use, regulation and treatment of water and land resources on a watershed to accomplish the stated objectives (*Soil Conservation Society of America*, 1982).
2. Watershed Management is the process of formulating and carrying out a course of action involving the manipulation of natural, agricultural and human resources in a watershed to provide goods and services that are desired by and suitable to the society, but under the condition that soil and water resources are not adversely affected. Watershed management must consider the social, economic and institutional factors operating within and outside the watershed (*Food and Agricultural Organization*, 1987).
3. Watershed Management is the harmonious development and management of land and water resources within the natural boundaries of a watershed, so as to promote or produce on a sustainable basis, abundance of plants and animals and their products and still deliver clean and controlled flow of water to the downstream (All India Soil and Land Use Survey, 1988).

From all the above definitions, it can be deduced that watershed management, in operational terms may be visualized as an endeavour towards proper utilization of land and water for augmenting agricultural production in private lands and other biomass production in degraded common and forest lands, in close cooperation with the local communities, so as to bring about a stable growth without causing environmental degradation. Since, resources are limited and needs are many, the available common resources are to be managed jointly by the communities themselves with due consideration for equity and social justice. Beginning essentially with the integrated land and water management, the process is not limited to these activities but also encompasses other related and supporting development activities such as development of rural energy, livestock, agro-processing, village amenities, credit societies, market linkages and so on.

In order to enable the communities to manage their own natural resources base more efficiently, development of skills and capabilities within the communities and creation of effective village level institutions are considered essential. Rural women in general and tribal women in particular depend heavily on natural resources in meeting the bulk of family needs like food, fuel, fodder, drinking water, etc. They have a greater stake in the regeneration and conservation of the environment. Hence, women not only need to be integrated in the community programmes but also should have greater decision-making power in planning and implementation.

Common Property Resources (CPRs) such as land, water, forest, fisheries, wildlife and agriculture constitute an important component of community assets in India and several other developing countries and significantly contribute towards the people's livelihoods despite the decline in their area and physical productivity. The poor households and small farmers secure a substantive portion of their fuel, fodder, income generation and risk minimizations through CPRs (Jodha, 2002).

Watershed management is required to enable a level of production sufficient to meet the needs of the present generation, without unduly degrading the natural resource base. The terms watershed management and watershed development are often considered synonymous and are used interchangeably. Management involves important functions like planning, organizing, controlling and monitoring, decision-making, etc. All these functions are essential for watershed management. Watershed development, on the other hand is understood as creation of physical structure to harness the natural resources within the boundary of a watershed apparently without giving much emphasis to the aspects of management of the same (M.K. Maitra, 2001).

India is an agrarian country where nearly 70 per cent of its population lives in rural area and depends directly on agriculture for its livelihood. Owing to the high pressure on land and the existing land ownership practices, the average size of the landholding is too small to make agriculture a profitable business. A majority of Indian farmers are engaged in subsistence farming. The common concerns that deserve national attention are issues associated with food security and efficient utilization of natural resources. These concerns require adoption of technologies that allow higher returns per unit application of inputs and promote the concept of value addition on the agriculture sector.

Of the total geographical area of our country, i.e. 329 m ha, the cultivated area is about 156 m ha which is about 49 per cent of the total area. This includes 143 m ha of net sown area and 14 m ha of current fallow. Of the cultivated land, about 53 million hectare (35%) is irrigated.

The remaining 90 million hectare is rainfed and the forest area is about 68 m ha (22%), the per capita land availability declined from 0.89 ha in 1951 to 0.37 ha in the mid 1990s and is estimated to reduce further to 0.19 ha by 2035. As far as agricultural land is concerned, the per capita availability of land is 0.48 ha only.

The main objective of a watershed development project is to achieve sustainable production of biomass and restoration of ecological balance in drought prone and rainfed areas, thereby improving people's standard of living. The specific objectives are Conservation, up-gradation and utilization of natural endowments, namely water and vegetation in a harmonious manner. Generation of large-scale employment during the project period and regular employment after project completion to enhance the work opportunities in backward rainfed areas with a view to ensuring livelihood security, particularly for the underprivileged sections of the rural population.

Improvement in the production environment and maintenance of the ecological balance through scientific management of land and rainwater, *in-situ* moisture conservation, introduction of a scientific production system, creation of a network of run-off management structures and devices for the recharge of groundwater for drinking purposes and domestic consumption and recycling of water for irrigation. It also aims at promotion of social forestry and horticulture activity in all suitable lands. Enhancement of the cash available with landless agricultural labourers and farmers through increased casual employment and marketable surplus of agricultural and dairy produce.

A watershed is termed as large, mini or micro depending on its size. This criterion has been evolved keeping in mind the size which can be managed for implementation by various project implementing agencies within a reasonable period. From the management point of view, a micro or small watershed is one which has a single drainage with its subsidiary branches extending to an area not more than 500 ha. A mini watershed is one which has the drainage system of less than 2000 ha and more than 500 ha. A large watershed is one which has an extent of more than 2,000 ha.

Historical Background

Integrated and participatory watershed development and management has emerged as the cornerstone of rural development in the dry and semi-arid regions of India. The programme initially launched to arrest the soil erosion in catchments of large and medium reservoirs, has since grown in scope. Watershed development today is one of the largest interventions in the country in terms of scale, resource allocation and agencies involved. Other than the Ministries of Rural Development (MoRD), specifically the Department of Land Resources (DoLR) and Ministry of Agriculture (MoA), the Ministry of Environment and Forests (MoEF) are also involved in watershed and economic development programmes.

The decade of the 1980s saw efforts to 'mainstream' successful experiments like Sukhomajri and Ralegaon Siddhi. While some community organizations/NGOs had already begun doing notable work in that area, the Government in 1982-83, started a programme in 19 locations under MoA to prepare water harvesting/conservation in rainfed areas. In 1984, the MoRD also initiated conservation strategies in 22 other locations with research and technology inputs from Indian Council of Agricultural Research (ICAR) to develop 41 model watersheds. In 1990, integrated watershed development was launched with the introduction of National Watershed Development Programme for Rainfed Areas (NWDPRA). Simultaneously, conservation programme was undertaken through the Drought Prone Area Programme (DPAP) initiated by MoRD in 1972-73 and the Desert Development Programme (DDP) initiated in 1977-78. Today, the major programmes include the Integrated Wasteland Development Programme (IWDP), River Valley Projects (RVPs) and Watershed Development Projects in Shifting Cultivation Areas (WDPSCA), among others.

In 1993, The Government of India constituted the C.H. Hanumantha Rao Committee to review the working of the watershed programmes under the Ministry of Rural Development. The committee advocated that a number of ongoing schemes like the Integrated Watershed Development Project (IWDP), Desert Development Programme (DDP) with common objectives such as soil and water conservation, wasteland development and drought proofing be consolidated as National Wasteland Development Programme (NWDP) funded and implemented by the Ministry of Rural Development (MoRD) in nearly 25 States across the country.

The development of ideas on sustainable livelihood was witnessed during 1990s. These grew from awareness that rural development approach based purely on agricultural production were insufficient to meet livelihood needs of the rural and landless poor. Agricultural land and livestock frequently generate only a portion of the rural livelihoods, which are not primarily agrarian or land based form of income generation.

This is supplemented by wage from labour, collection of Non-Timber Forest Produce (NTFP), part time trade and handicraft production to their income. Instead of considering land or water and its potential for development attention was given instead to people's needs and their priorities for development, which is challenging for land based development projects such as the watershed development programme.

As the international development goals have widened from merely increasing food production to include poverty reduction and environmental sustainability, protection of the environment is a big challenge for developing nations, and greater emphasis should be given to check the exploitation of the natural resources base. Soil erosion and land degradation coupled with declining per capita availability of land and freshwater are posing serious threat to environment. This is becoming more intense with burgeoning population causing food security problems in developing countries. Hence, careful and concerted efforts are needed for efficient and effective management of natural resources for increased productivity for the soils.

Several Government and non-governmental agencies have launched watershed development projects to tackle some of these generic problems with the objectives of soil conservation, improving the land productivity and promoting appropriate technologies for efficient and sustainable use of natural resources. However, many watershed projects around the world have not performed well because of the poor community participation (Johnson *et al.*, 2001). The key to the success of any watershed project and its sustainability depends on the people's participation for achieving the desired participation of people, the role of the community organizations, groups and other stakeholders are crucial. Local community must play an active role starting from project design to implementation and maintenance of the project. In this context, a participatory watershed development approach is considered as ideal for achieving food security and sustainability. Participatory watershed management has emerged as a new paradigm for sustainable rural livelihoods and it occupies the centre stage of rural development in the fragile and semi-arid environments of developing nations. The concept of participatory watershed development emphasizes an interdisciplinary, intersectoral and multi-institutional mechanism (Rhodes and Elliot). Participatory watershed management has been defined as a process "which aims to create a self-supporting system, which is essential for sustainability" (Wani *et al.*, 2005). Participatory watershed management provides opportunity to stakeholders to jointly negotiate their interests, set priorities, evaluate opportunities, implement and monitor the outcomes. This concept came widely into practice in late 1980s and over the time people's institutions like Zilla Parishads (ZPs), Self-Help Groups (SHGs), and watershed implementing committees were gradually involved in the project management system. With allocation of more funds for watershed development, several non-governmental organizations came forward to aggressively participate in implementing the watershed programmes.

In India, participatory watershed management has its roots in the non-governmental sector that go back nearly as far as the government programmes. The seeds of the participatory watershed management can be traced to a small village called Ralegaon Siddhi in Maharashtra of India. Anna Hazare, a local leader was responsible for bringing many social changes in village particularly soil and water conservation measures besides family planning, a ban on alcohol, protection of non-arable lands against open grazing and felling of trees and voluntary labour for the community welfare and other measures which helped in natural resources base of the village (Kerr *et al.*, 2002). This ultimately led to people participation in watershed management and the evolution of participatory watershed management looking beyond just the bio-physical aspects to focus on social and institutional aspects following a bottom up approach. It is now accepted that the communities must participate to enhance the productivity of natural resources in a sustainable fashion (Turton *et al.*, 1998).

Three Ministries at the national level are involved in watershed and eco-development programmes namely, Department of Land Resources (MoLR), Department of Agriculture and Cooperation (MoA), and Ministry of Environment and Forests (MoEF). Besides planned allocation of resources, these Ministries also implement externally aided projects. As of March 2005, the MoA had treated an area of 17.24 m ha at the cost of ₹ 9,368.03 crore and MoRD had treated 27.52 m ha at an outlay of ₹ 6,855.66 crore. Some of the major programmes of MoRD are DPAP, DDP, IWDP and that of MoA is National Watershed Development Programme for Rainfed Areas (NWDPRA), River Valley Projects (RVP) and Watershed Development Projects in Shifting Cultivation Area (WDPSCA), etc. The National Bank for Agriculture and Rural Development (NABARD) and the Department of Agriculture and Cooperation (MoA) established the development fund with an initial corpus of ₹ 200 crore. There are also a number of State sponsored, bilateral and privately funded projects implemented by a large number of agencies and NGOs. Watershed development has today virtually became the flagship programme of rural development in India, with an estimated annual expenditure of ₹ 2,300 crore during the Tenth Plan (GoI, 2006) and a target of treating 63 million ha over the next 20-25 years with an estimated outlay of ₹ 76,000 crore (GoI, 2000). It is no longer seen as an experiment, but accepted by Government, Donors and NGOs alike, as a core strategy that subsumes all other activities, such as afforestation or common land regeneration and stabilizes rural livelihoods through its multi-sectoral approach, especially in the dry and rainfed regions of India (A. Samuel, *et al.*, 2008).

The Government of India accorded high priority on watershed development projects. It can be counted among the foremost nations to have taken note of problems of soil erosion and land degradation with the initiation of planned development in 1951. Soil and water conservation practices have been accepted as one of the important inputs for increasing agricultural productivity of the country. In order to check soil erosion, soils and water conservation programmes were launched both under State as well as Central sectors during the Five Year Plans. While the conceptual framework of soil and water conservation practices has not altered, the concept of programmes has undergone considerable revision during successive Five Year Plans.

Main aims of the projects in operation are:

- To minimize the process of erosion and land degradation to restore degraded lands.
- To ensure availability of water and soil moisture.
- To create micro-level irrigation potential through water harvesting.
- To increase aggregate bio-mass production.
- To generate employment through continuous adjustments in optimum land use planning.
- To ensure collective security against recurring droughts and floods.

The schemes under the State Government aims at conservation of soil and water on agricultural lands with some components of land reclamation, soil and land use survey and plantation of utility trees on private and public lands. The programmes sponsored by the Government of India provide an overall perspective of the problems such as water and wind erosion, degradation through waterlogging, salinity, ravines, torrents, shifting cultivation, coastal sands in addition to the declining rain-land ratio, increasing and competing favourable provision of water into production system as well as its information on problems and potential of various land uses. Dhurva Narayana and others discussed the various soil and water conservation programmes initiated by the Central and State Governments over the years. Some of the important programmes are discussed below:

(a) *Soil Conservation in Catchments of River Valley Projects:* This programme was initiated during the Third Five Year Plan. The objective was to treat the catchment area for reducing silt production rate and subsequent siltation of reservoir. It also assisted to improve the productivity of the catchments by checking soil erosion. This programme is being implemented in 27 watersheds covering 17 States including Damodar Valley Corporation area. Soil and water conservation measures are being adopted in critically degraded watersheds ranging from 2,000 to 4,000 ha of land. These watersheds are being delineated by All India Soil and Land Use Survey Organization. The programme has got in-built facilities for collecting silt load data along with different characteristics of watersheds under treatment.

(b) *Integrated Watershed Management in Catchments of Flood Prone Rivers:* This programme was launched during the Fourth Five Year Plan in eight flood prone rivers of Gangetic basin namely Ajoy, Gomti, Punpun, Sahibi, Sone, Upper Ganga and Upper Yamuna. The total area of the watershed is 16.7 million ha and covers parts of the States of Bihar, Haryana, Himachal Pradesh, Madhya Pradesh, Rajasthan, Uttar Pradesh, West Bengal and Union Territory of Delhi. The programme aims at the enhancing ability of the watershed by absorbing larger quantity of rain-water, reducing erosion and consequent silt load in rivers and thus assisting in mitigating the fury of floods in productive plains.

(c) *Drought Prone Area Programme (DPAP):* The Drought Prone Area Programme was started in 1973 as an integrated area programme. This programme was considered as a long-term measure for restoration of ecological balance by conserving, developing and harnessing land, water and livestock and human resources. The aims of the programme are to minimize the adverse affects of drought on production of crops and livestock and productivity of land, water and human resources through integrated development of natural resource base of the areas and adoption of appropriate technologies and to conserve, develop and harness land, water and other natural resources including rainfall for restoration of ecological balance in the long run. The DPAP operates in 615 blocks of 95 districts in 13 States. The total area covered by the scheme is 53.6 m ha.

(d) *Desert Development Programme (DDP):* The Desert Development Programme was initiated in 1977-78 with the objective of controlling desertification of desert areas through integrating and dovetailing other related State and Central programmes and to conserve, develop and harness land, water and other natural resources including rainfall restoration of ecological balance in the long-run. The aims of the programme are to be achieved through activities like afforestation with special emphasis on sand dune stabilization and shelter belt plantation and grassland development. This programme covers 131 blocks of 21 districts in five States namely Rajasthan, Haryana, Gujarat (hot arid region), Jammu & Kashmir and Himachal Pradesh (cold arid region). The total area covered by the DDP is about 32.6 m ha. This programme is implemented with cent per cent Central assistance.

(e) *Himalayan Watershed Management Project in Uttar Pradesh:* This programme was initiated in 1983 with the financial assistance of the World Bank. The aims of the project were to minimize further deterioration of Himalayan ecosystem caused by depletion of forest cover, overgrazing, bad land use and careless road construction. Two watersheds namely Nayar in Garhwal and Panar in Kumaon regions covered total of 2.47 lakh ha.

(f) *Operational Research Projects on Integrated Watershed Management:* These projects were initiated in 1983-84 with financial assistance of Ministry of Agriculture and Rural Development, Government of India and under the technical guidance of Indian Council of Agricultural Research (ICAR). The objectives of this project were to develop a programme with people's participation and arresting the deterioration of environment and building up permanent assets in the form of water, sustainable vegetation and improved productivity of cropped land. The projects cover as many as 47 watersheds (17 with the Central Soil and Water Conservation and Research and Training Institute, Dehradun and 30 with Central Research Institute for Dry Land Agriculture, Hyderabad). These projects were spread over 16 States namely Andhra Pradesh, Bihar, Gujarat, Haryana, Madhya Pradesh, Maharashtra, Odisha, Punjab, Himachal Pradesh,

Jammu and Kashmir, Karnataka, Kerala, Rajasthan, Tamil Nadu, Uttar Pradesh and West Bengal. The project covered a total area of 35,739 ha in most of the watershed surface and underground water resources have been created. Significant increase in water storage and recycling of stored water accomplished in most of the watersheds for production of crops. *In-situ* moisture conservation techniques like contour cultivation, mulching, flat on-grade ridging systems, bed furrow system, off season tillage, etc. have been demonstrated at the farmers' field. Even in the conditions of severe drought the effects of watershed has minimized hardship in the watershed areas (Dhurva Narayan *et al.*, 1987).

(g) *National Wasteland Development Project for Rainfed Areas (NWDPRA):* The NWDPRA programme was initiated in 1986-87. This programme is being implemented in the un-irrigated arable lands falling in the rainfall range 500 to 1,125 mm. The programme covers 25 States and the district with more than 30 per cent of area under irrigation is usually excluded. In the Eighth Five Year Plan, the NWDPRA was restructured to achieve the twin objectives of sustainable production of bio-mass and restoration of ecological balance in the vast rainfed areas of the country.

(h) *Integrated Wasteland Development Project (Hills):* The Integrated Wasteland Development Project (Hills) is being implemented with the assistance of World Bank. It is operating in Himachal Pradesh, Jammu and Kashmir, Punjab and Haryana. It covers total area of 1.24 lakh ha. The aims of the project are to slow and reverse degradation of the natural environment through the use of appropriate soil and water conservation practices.

(i) *Integrated Watershed Development Project (Plains):* This programme is being implemented with the assistance of the World Bank in Gujarat, Odisha, Rajasthan. It covers an area of 4.33 lakh ha. The aims of the project are to slowdown and possibly reverse ecological degradation in a variety of agro-ecological zones by promoting sustainable and replicable production system.

(j) *Integrated Agricultural Development in Drought Prone Areas:* The dry farming areas in India constituted about 19 per cent of the total cultivated area of the country. Subsistence farming is practiced in dry farming regions with the farmers depending on the vagaries of the weather. The resulting human suffering when the monsoon has failed has been the main reason for initiating many drought relief programmes by the Central Government. The Drought Prone Area Programme (DPAP) was envisaged to promote integrated agricultural development in dry farming on the lines recommended by the task force of the Planning Commission (1973). The task force called for a radical departure from the unproductive and palliative aspects of drought relief and for the working out of an ecologically balanced approach for integrated agricultural development of the dry farming regions of the country. The task force made some concrete suggestions to extend the benefits of dry farming research results through a planned programme of action in project context with a master plan and detailed annual plans worked out on an area basis. Depending on the exigencies of the drought, these could be conceived as productive infrastructure investments in case of emergencies in order to provide immediate employment to the weaker sections of the society. The task force felt that such a useful orientation should come about in DPAP through planning methodology where there is a detailed soil survey, hydrological survey and topographic survey is essential prerequisites for preparation of the master plan. Based on these surveys, the task force stated that the land use capabilities are to be decided and works such as the types of well to be sunk, water harvesting structures such as construction of tanks or check dams in the catchment areas, etc. are to be planned not only to mitigate the effects of drought themselves but also to improve the ecology of the entire area. This implies that lands not suitable for agriculture are to be put under pasture and forestry to enhance their positive ecological impact. The task force has also recognized that high water use efficiency has to be build into the programmes of action of DPAP. Water is very scarce in these areas and it is usually available from wells only. It is therefore important that the full potential of the underground water is exploited keeping rates of renewability in view so as to support intensive farming of fertile arable lands. Provision should be made so that supplementary irrigation facility is available to the community as a whole instead of the few influential cultivators and the total production is enhanced substantially. This strategy calls for application of water at critical stages of the crops.

Integrated agricultural development in drought prone area can be achieved through comprehensive programme planning with a broad strategy in terms of promoting a productive infrastructure, promotion of efficient water use with equitable distribution of renewable water resources, reorientation of cropping pattern and agricultural enterprise (including forestry) to bring down the level of risk in dry farming tracts to acceptable levels and back-up of the cropping pattern envisaged by an integrated approach to input credit supplies appropriate to the socio-resource dimension of micro-regions (Ratnam, 1980).

(k) *Other Watershed Management Projects:* In addition to the above mentioned projects many other watershed development projects with externally aided projects are being in operation, e.g. Japan, Germany, Sweden and international organizations like, Food and Agricultural Organization (FAO), United Nations Development Fund (UNDP), World Bank, European Economic Council (EEC), etc. are being implemented in the country.

The huge investment in watershed development projects is justifiable if it enhances productivity of rainfed areas. Even though there is paucity of reliable, scientific and methodologically rigorous research and studies, those that have been undertaken show that many projects have created positive impacts in terms of the increased water availability, agricultural productivity and rural employment. Sustenance of these impacts is also a critical area on which information is not readily available. As the country is progressing towards a new generation of watershed development (post-Hariyali and the Common Guidelines approach to watershed development), with high expectations and large scale targets, it is important that experiences and learning are studied and consolidated of the projects that are being widely as well as innovatively implemented during the past two and a half decades, especially after the 1990, 1994 and 2003 guidelines.

Water Management Structures

The creation of water management structures followed the ridge to valley approach. The identification of various type of water management structures required at a particular place depends on the felt need of the village community. Various types of water management structures used for controlling and minimizing the erosion are as follows:

(i) *Loose Boulder Structure (LBS):* These structures are constructed in upper reaches of the hillock as part of the catchments treatment. The purpose of this structure is to obstruct flow of rainwater with stone boulders of various sizes and shapes to check the velocity of water, which considerably reduces the force of gushing water. As a result of this, large volume of rainwater reaches to agricultural fields.

(ii) *Gully Plugging:* Gully plugs are built with loose stone and cement to reduce the velocity of run-off water in *nalas*. It is constructed to minimize erosion of soil so that cultivable land could be protected from run-off water.

(iii) *Continuous Contour Trench (CCT):* CCT is a device by which the velocity of the run-off water is checked through the digging of trenches. CCTs are constructed around the hill slopes at a given contour for treating non-arable area of hill slopes. Trench which is dug on contour lines is called as contour trench. When the trenches are continuous it is known as continuous contour trench.

(iv) *Check Dam:* Check Dams are constructed across the direction of the water flow on shallow rivers and streams for the purpose of water harvesting. The dams retained excess water flow during monsoon rains in a small catchment area behind the structure. Pressure created in the catchment area helped force the impounded water reaching to the agricultural field in the non-monsoon seasons.

(v) *Diversion Channel:* In the sloppy area the run-off water in the rainy season enter into fields of farmers and damages the crops. Diversion channels are constructed to check the direct run-off water that hits agricultural field and causes the soil erosion. As a result the run-off water gradually enters into the fields of farmers through an outlet.

The selection of watershed may be done on priority basis considering the following aspects:

- Watershed having acute shortage of drinking water.
- Watershed with large population of SCs/STs.
- Watershed which has preponderance of wastelands.
- Watershed where actual wages are significantly lower than the minimum wages.
- Watershed which is contiguous to another developed/selected watershed for development.
- Watershed where community is actively interested in taking up the area development on a watershed basis and willing to make necessary local contributions.

Priority Delineation and Codification of Watersheds: One of the first requisites for planning is to delineate and codify the catchments of the country into watersheds and sub-watersheds. The All India Soil and Land Use Survey Organization is doing this through the development of a national watershed Atlas. In all, 3537 watersheds have been identified in 35 basins, 125 catchments and 500 sub-catchments. Priority delineation method developed and improved over the decades has used weighted Silt Yield Index (SYI) for each of the watershed computed from weighted erosion intensity and adjusted by delivery ratio. The All India Soil and Land Use Survey is the organization that has been carrying out test studies for application of remote sensing technology for catchment characteristics particularly with reference to soil erosion, treatment yield and prioritization of watersheds.

Stages of Watershed Development Programmes

The implementation of watershed development programme can be divided into four stages, i.e. preparatory, planning, implementation and withdrawal stage. In the first stage, preliminary PRA exercises are conducted to identify the needs of the community and decide about the Entry Point Activities (EPAs). The focus is on gaining an entry into the community and spreading awareness among the people the scientific basis of watershed as an ecological system, which links one farmer to others. The planning stage involves demarcation of the watershed areas and specific points were the treatment in the watershed has to be done. Here the involvement of the stakeholders is essential in social mapping and deciding upon the strategies of intervention. The implementation stage includes strengthening the community organization in the watershed area. The institutions that are strengthened are the Mahila Mandals, Panchayats, Yuvak Sanghs, Self-Help Groups, etc. It involves building of watershed structures and contributions are in the form of land, labour and money. Arrangements for management of Common Property Resources (CPR) through user groups and watershed management committee are also made. The last stage of the policy comprises handing over the project to the community. This stage concentrates on the capacity building of the community people, so that they can completely takeover the maintenance of the watershed structures and institutions. As such, people's participation gives the project its much needed sustainability especially when the interventions aims at an integrated approach linking it to developmental objectives of a rural area.

Benefits of Watershed Management

The watershed programmes produce multiple tangible and intangible benefits for individuals and community as a whole. The present generation watershed programmes are not only conserving but also augmenting water and land resources, increasing agricultural and livestock productivity, enhancing incomes, protecting and providing environmental services, promoting collective action and addressing issues of women and equity for vulnerable groups through development of social capital and institutions, including building resilience of natural and human resources to cope with the future changes including those due to climate change. Therefore, watershed management has been a key component of development planning of rainfed drought prone area since the early 1980s.

Participatory Approach: Experiences have shown that the sustainability of watershed projects is closely linked to effective participation of the communities who derive their living from natural resources. Active people's participation is a prerequisite for the success of watershed development programmes. Involvement of local stake-holders in planning, development and execution of watershed activity is crucial. The watershed is a community development approach and hence it calls for community participation and collective action. It is necessary because individual choices have collective consequences in the watershed framework. Action of one group of farmers in one location affects adversely or favourably another group of farmers in a different location (off-site impact). Such externalities influence the performance of the watershed at large. Often the different groups and locations have conflicting objectives with respect to their investment enterprise choices. These need to be converted into opportunities. The action of all the farmers in the watershed should converge in such a way that the positive externalities are maximized and negative externalities are minimized. To achieve this, the community or stakeholder has to develop their own rules, which resolve their conflicting objectives. It is believed that better organized and effective people's participation would yield higher benefits (P.K. Joshi, *et al.*, 2008).

The first generation watershed programmes in the country were supply driven. The Government official used to identify the location and decide various activities for implementation of watershed programmes, which were funded by Central and State Governments. The top-down approach did not match the needs of the stakeholders in the watershed.

In the absence of people's participation, the potential benefits of watershed programmes could not be realized. To overcome this problem, the concept of Participatory Integrated Development of Watershed (PIDOW) was initiated in 1980s. However, only a partial success could be achieved, and some radical steps were taken to involve the local stakeholders/people in planning, formulation and implementation of watershed programmes in the country. In due course, the people's institutions, such as Zilla Parishad, Self-Help Groups and watershed implementing committees gradually involved in the project management system. With more funds allocated for watershed development, several NGOs were involved in the project and they emphasized on the importance of people's involvement in the successes of the watersheds. Most of the arrangements were informal and varied across watersheds and implementing agencies. To make it formal, the 1994 watershed guidelines specifically included people's involvement as one of the conditions in the watershed development. It is important that people involve themselves voluntarily and not forcefully. It is, therefore, important to find out conditions under which the watershed beneficiaries would involve themselves in implementation, during the project tenure and maintenance of structure after the project is formally over. The watershed that involves activities which are able to cater to the specific needs of the local people certainly attracts higher people's participation. It is, therefore, essential to ensure that once the watershed is identified, the need of the stakeholders must be assessed together by the implementing agency and the stakeholders. Since, a watershed has a diversify group of beneficiaries, all genuine and valid needs of each and every group should be appropriately addressed in the watershed. At times, it has been observed that in many watersheds only influential and large farmers were involved and the small and marginal farmers have been left out. Besides, there was evidence that the most of the watersheds are not sensitive to the needs of the women and landless labourers. Often the women and landless labourers were silently left out of the watershed related decision-making process (Meinzen-Dick, *et al.*, 2004).

In spite of a bottom-up approach for planning and implementation of a watershed development, community participation was not forthcoming in most of the watershed programmes. The main reason for the low or contractual mode of participation was that large number of small and marginal farmers was not getting tangible economic benefits as productivity enhancement initiatives were missing to a large extent.

In most watershed programmes, Entry Point Activity (EPA) as identified by the community is undertaken under the project to build rapport with the community through activities such as construction of a meeting room, school, classroom, borewell, pump, drinking water tank, etc.

Guidelines for the Establishment of Watershed Development Programmes

The Government of India at various points of time has framed guidelines for the establishment of watershed development programmes in various parts of the country. The various guidelines provided by the Central Government from time to time are discussed briefly.

In the year 1994, a technical committee under the Chairmanship of Prof. C.H. Hanumantha Rao, was appointed to assess the Drought Prone Area Programme (DPAP) and the Desert Development Programme (DDP) with the purpose of identifying weaknesses and providing suggestions for improvements. The committee after careful appraisal, opined that the "the programmes have been implemented in a fragmented manner by different departments through rigid guidelines without any well designed plans prepared on the watershed basis by involving the inhabitants. Except in a few places, the achievements have been sub-optimal. Ecological degradation has been proceeding unabated in these areas with reduced forest cover, reducing water table and shortage of drinking water, fuel and fodder" (Hanumantha Rao Committee, 1994, preface).

Against this backdrop, the committee made a number of recommendations and formulated a set of guidelines that brought the DDP, the DPAP and the Integrated Wasteland Development Programme (IWDP) under a single umbrella. The watershed development programmes taken up by the Ministry of Rural Development (MoRD) from 1994 to 2001 followed these guidelines. In the year 2000, the Ministry of Agriculture revised its guidelines for its programme, the National Watershed Development Project for Rainfed Areas (NWDPRA). These guidelines were intended to be common guidelines to make the programme more participatory, sustainable and equitable. However, the MoRD revised 1994 Hanumantha Rao Committee guidelines in 2001 and yet again in 2003 under the nomenclature "Hariyali Guidelines".

The Hariyali Guidelines

The Hariyali Guidelines is meant to simplify the procedure and involve the Panchayati Raj Institutions (PRIs) more meaningfully in planning, implementation and management of economic development activities in rural areas. These new guidelines were issued in the year 2003.

The objectives of projects under HARIYALI were:

- Harvesting every drop of rainwater for the purpose of irrigation, plantation including Horticulture and Floriculture, pasture development, fisheries, etc. to create sustainable source of income for the village community as well as for drinking water supplies.
- Ensuring overall development of rural areas through the gram panchayats and creating regular sources of income for the panchayats for the rainwater harvesting and management.
- Employment generation, poverty alleviation, community empowerment and development of human and other economic resources of the rural areas.
- Mitigating the adverse effects of extreme climatic conditions such as drought and desertification on crops, human and livestock population for the overall improvement of rural areas.
- Restoring ecological balance by harnessing, conserving and developing natural resources, i.e. land, water, vegetative cover and especially plantations.
- Encouraging village community towards sustained community action for the operation and maintenance of assets created and further development of the potential of the natural resources of the watershed.
- Potential use of simple, easy and affordable technological solutions and institutional arrangements that make use of and build upon, local technical knowledge and available materials.

In the Hariyali Guideline the broad criteria followed for the selection of the watersheds were:

- Watersheds where people's participation is assured through contribution of labour, material, etc. for the development as well as for the operation and maintenance of the assets created.
- Watershed areas having acute shortage of drinking water.
- Watersheds having large population of Scheduled Castes/ Scheduled Tribe population.

- Watershed having a preponderance of non-forest wastelands/degraded lands.
- Watersheds having preponderance of common lands.
- Watersheds where actual wages are significantly lower than the minimum wages.
- Watershed which is contiguous to another watershed that has already been developed/treated.

Watershed area may be of an average size of 500 hectare, preferably covering an entire village. However, if on actual survey, a watershed is found to have less or more area, the total area may be taken up for development as a project.

In order to assess the performance of various ongoing projects/programmes of the watershed development, a series of evaluation studies have been conducted by Indian Council of Agriculture Research (ICAR) institute, State Agricultural Universities, National Remote Sensing Agency (NRSA), etc. Besides impact assessment studies were taken up by the Ministry of Agriculture, Ministry of Rural Development, Planning Commission, International Crop Research Institute for Semi Arid Tropics (ICRISAT) and the technical committee constituted by the Department of Land Resources (DoLR). These studies support the observation that in several watersheds, the implementation of the programme has been effective for natural resource conservation by increasing the productivity of the land, bringing additional area under agriculture, employment generation and social upliftment of beneficiaries living in rural areas. But these successes have been sporadic and intermittent. The overall impact at the state and national levels has generally been inadequate. Additional demand and supply driven socio-economic and risk managing paradigms are emerging (Common Guidelines for Watershed Development Projects).

It is in this context that in coordination with the Planning Commission an initiative has been taken to formulate "Common Guidelines for Watershed Development Projects" in order to have a unified perspective by all Ministries. These guidelines are, therefore, applicable to all watershed development projects in all departments/ministries of Government of India concerned with Watershed Development Projects.

The Common Guidelines

The key features of the new guidelines known as the Common Guidelines can be broadly outlined as follows:

(a) *Delegation of Power to States:* States will now be empowered to sanction and oversee the implementation of the watershed projects within their jurisdiction and within the parameters set out in these guidelines.

(b) *Dedicated Institutions:* There would be dedicated implementing agencies with multi-disciplinary professional teams at the national, state and district level for managing the watershed programmes.

(c) *Financial Assistance to Dedicated Institutions:* Additional financial assistance would be provided for strengthening of the institutions at the district, state and national level to ensure professionalism in management of watershed projects.

(d) *Duration of the Programme:* With the expanded scope and expectations under this approach, the project duration has been enhanced in the range of 4 years to 7 years depending on the nature of the activities spread over three distinct phases, i.e. preparatory phase, works phase and consolidation phase.

(e) *Livelihood Orientation:* Productivity enhancement and livelihoods shall be given priority along with conservation measures. Resource development and usage will be planned to promote farming and allied activities to promote local livelihoods while ensuring resource conservation and regeneration. The new approach would systematically integrate livestock and fisheries management as a Central intervention and encourage dairying and marketing of dairy products. In the rainfed areas, the animal resources become a major source of income for the people. When effectively integrated with watershed development, a comprehensive animal husbandry component would contribute significantly to ensure a better and sustainable livelihood for the people of rainfed areas.

(f) *Cluster Approach:* The new approach envisages a broader vision of geo-hydrological units normally of average size of 1,000 to 5,000 hectares comprising of cluster of micro-watershed. If resources and area exist additional watershed in contiguous areas in clusters may be taken up. However, smaller size projects will be sanctioned in hilly/difficult areas.

(g) *Scientific Planning:* Special efforts need to be made to utilize the information and technology and remote sensing inputs in planning, monitoring and evaluation of the programme.

(h) *Capacity-building:* Capacity-building and training of all functionaries and stakeholders involved in the watershed programme implementation would be carried out on war footing with definite action plan and requisite professionalism and competence.

(i) *Multi-tier Approach:* There would be a multi-tier ridge to valley sequenced approach, which should be adopted towards implementation of the watershed development projects. The higher reaches or the forests are actually where the water sources originate. The approach, therefore is to identify an area, and first look at the forest and hilly regions, in the upper catchments wherever possible. In the upper reaches which is the most hilly and forested, the implementation would mainly lie with the forest departments and Joint Forest Management Committees (JFMC).

The second-tier is the intermediate tier or the slopes, which are just above the agricultural lands. In the intermediate slopes, the watershed management approach would address all the necessary issues by looking at all the best possible options including treatment, cropping pattern, horticulture, agro-forestry, etc.

The third-tier constitutes the plains and flat areas, where typically the farmers are operating; there would be a large concentration of labour intensive works. The watershed development process would be synergized with the employment generating programmes such as the National Rural Employment Guarantee Scheme (NREGS), Backward Regions Grant Funds (BRGF), etc.

Institutional Arrangements at National, State and District Levels

For effective implementation of the watershed development programmes the common guidelines suggests the following institutional arrangements at various levels.

(a) *Role of National Rainfed Area Authority (NRAA):* The NRAA would be responsible for supporting the preparation of strategic plans for watershed based development projects at the State and district levels keeping in view specific agro-climatic and socio-economic conditions. It also assists in the preparation of the State specific technical manuals for the multi-disciplinary and integrated approach required for the implementation of these projects together with standards and specifications, etc. It is also responsible for action research relevant to watershed development programme in different agro-climatic regions. The NRAA conducts studies, evaluation and impact assessments from time-to-time so, that the benefits of these are available for improving the quality of watershed management projects. It also facilitates convergence of different schemes and projects of Government of India which are having similar objectives. The other important responsibilities are organizing regional and international conferences, seminars and workshops, study tours and information sharing. It also provides technical knowledge inputs and expertise for the management of WDPs.

(b) *State Level Nodal Agency (SLNA):* A dedicated State Level Nodal Agency (SLNA) will be constituted by the State Government having an independent bank account. The main functions of the SLNA will be to:

- Prepare a perspective and strategic plan of watershed development for the State on the basis of plans prepared at the block and district level and indicate implementation strategy and expected outputs/outcomes, financial outlays and approach the nodal agency at the Central level in the department for appraisal and clearance.
- Establish and maintain a State level data cell from the funds sanctioned to the States, and connect it online with the national level data centre.
- Provide technical support to District Watershed Development Units (DWDUs) throughout the State.
- Approve a list of institutions for capacity-building of various stakeholders within the State and workout the overall capacity-building strategy in consultation with NRAA/nodal Ministry.
- Approve Project Implementing Agencies identified/ selected by DWDU/ District Level committee by adopting appropriate objective selection criteria and transparent systems.
- Establish monitoring, evaluation and learning systems at various levels.
- Ensure regular and quality online monitoring of watershed projects in the State in association with Nodal Agency at the Central level and securing feedback by developing partnership with independent and capable agencies.

(c) *District Watershed Development Unit (DWDU):* At the district level, where the area under watershed development projects is about 25,000 hectare, a separate dedicated unit, called District Watershed Development Unit (DWDU) will be established which will oversee the implementation of watershed programme in each district and will have separate independent accounts for this purpose.

The DWDU will be a separate unit with full time Project Manager and 3 to 4 subject matter specialists on Agriculture/Water Management/ Social Mobilization/Management and Accountants appointed on the basis of their qualification and expertise on contract/deputation/transfer, etc.

The functions of DWDU will be as follows:

(i) Identify potential Project Implementing Agencies (PIAs) in consultation with SLNA as per the empanelment process as decided by the respective State Governments.
(ii) Take up the overall responsibility of facilitating the preparation of strategic and annual action plans for watershed development projects in respective districts.
(iii) Providing professional technical support to Project Implementing Agencies (PIAs) in planning and execution of watershed development projects.
(iv) Develop action plans for capacity-building, with close involvement of resource organizations to execute the capacity-building action plans.
(v) Carry out regular monitoring, evaluation and learning.
(vi) Ensure smooth flow of funds to the watersheds.
(vii) Facilitate coordination with relevant programmes of agriculture, horticulture, rural development, animal husbandry, etc. with watershed development projects for enhancement of productivity and livelihoods.
(viii) Integrate watershed development projects/plans into district plans of district planning committees. All expenditure of watershed project would be reflected in district plans.
(ix) Establish and maintain the District Level Data Cell and link it with the State and national level data centre.

Institutional Arrangement at the Project Level

(i) *Project Implementing Agency (PIA):* The State Level Nodal Agency would evolve appropriate mechanism for selecting and approving the PIAs, who would be responsible for implementation of the watershed projects in different districts. These PIAs may include relevant line departments, autonomous organizations under State and Central Governments, Government Institutes/Research Bodies, Intermediate Panchayats, Voluntary Organizations (VOs). The PIAs should preferably have prior experience in watershed related aspects or management of watershed development projects and they should be prepared to constitute dedicated watershed development teams.

Roles and Responsibilities of the PIAs

(a) The Project Implementing Agency (PIA) will provide necessary technical guidance to the Gram Panchayats for preparation of development plans for the watershed through the Participatory Rural Appraisal (PRA) exercise, undertake community organization and training for the village communities, supervise watershed development activities, inspect and authenticate project accounts, encourage adoption of low cost technologies and build upon indigenous technical knowledge, monitor and review the overall project implementation and set-up institutional arrangements for post-project operation and maintenance and further development of assets created during the project period.

(b) The PIA, after careful scrutiny, shall submit the action plan for Watershed Development Project for approval of DWDU/DRDA and other arrangements. The PIA shall submit the periodical progress report to DWDU. The PIA shall also arrange physical, financial and social audit of the work undertaken. It will facilitate the mobilization of additional financial resources from other Government programmes, such as NREGA, BRGF, SGRY, National Horticulture Mission, Tribal Welfare Schemes, Artificial Ground Water Recharging, Green India, etc.

(ii) *Watershed Development Team (WDT):* The watershed development team is an integral part of the PIA and will be set up by the PIA. Each WDT should have at least four members, broadly with knowledge and experience in agriculture, soil science, water management, social mobilization and institutional building. At least one member of the WDT should be a woman. The WDT members should preferably have a professional degree. The WDT should be located as close as possible to the watershed project. The WDT should function in close collaboration with the team of experts at the district and state level.

Roles and Responsibilities of the WDT: The main role and responsibility of the WDT are as follows:

(a) Assist Gram Panchayat/Gram Sabha in constitution of the watershed committee and their functioning.
(b) Organizing and nurturing User Groups and Self-Help Groups.
(c) Mobilizing women to ensure that the perspective and interests of women are adequately reflected in the watershed action plan.
(d) Conducting the participatory base-line surveys, training and capacity building.
(e) Preparing detailed resource development plans including water and soil conservation or reclamation, etc. to promote sustainable livelihood at household level.
(f) Preparing Detailed Project Report (DPR) for the consideration of Gram Sabha.
(g) Common property resource management and equitable sharing.
(h) Undertake engineering surveys, prepare engineering drawings and cost estimates for structures to be built.
(i) Monitoring, checking, assessing, and undertaking physical verification and measurement of work done.
(j) Facilitating the development of livelihood opportunities for the landless.
(k) Arranging physical, financial and social audit of the work undertaken.
(l) Setting up suitable arrangements for post-project operation, maintenance and future development of the assets created during the project period.

Institutional Arrangements at the Village Level and People's Participation

(i) Self-Help Groups (SHGs): The Watershed Committee (WC) shall constitute SHGs in the watershed area with the help of WDT from amongst poor, small and marginal farmer households, landless/assetless poor agricultural labourers, women, and shepherd and SC/ST persons. These groups shall be homogenous groups having common identity and interest who are dependent on watershed area for their livelihood. Each self-help group will be provided with a revolving fund of an amount to be decided by the nodal Ministry.

(ii) User Groups (UGs): The watershed Committee (WC) shall also constitute User Groups in the watershed area with the help of WDT. These shall be homogenous group of persons most affected by each work/activity and shall include those having landholdings within the watershed area. Each User Group shall consist of those who are likely to derive direct benefits from a particular watershed work or activity. The WC with the help of the WDT shall facilitate resource use agreements among the user groups based on the principle of equity and sustainability. These agreements must be worked out before the concerned work is undertaken. It must be regarded as a pre-condition for that activity. The User Groups will be responsible for the operation and maintenance of all the assets created under the project in close collaboration with the Gram Sabha.

(iii) Watershed Committee (WC): The Gram Sabha will constitute the Watershed Committee (WC) to implement the watershed project with the technical support of the WDT in the village. The Watershed Committee has to be registered under the Society Registration Act, 1860. The Gram Sabha may elect/appoint any suitable person from village as the Chairman of Watershed Committee. The Committee will comprise of at least 10 members, half of the members shall be representatives of SHGs and User Groups, SC/ST community, women and landless persons in the village. One member of the WDT shall also be represented in the Watershed Committee (WC).

The Watershed Committee will open a separate bank account to receive funds for watershed projects and will utilize the same for undertaking its activities. The expense towards the salaries of the WDT members and Secretary of Watershed Committee shall be charged from the administrative expenses under professional support to the PIA.

(iv) Secretary, Watershed Committee: The Secretary, Watershed Committee will be selected in a meeting of the Gram Sabha. This person would be an independent paid functionary distinct and separate from the Panchayat Secretary. He would be a dedicated functionary with no responsibility other than the assistance to the Watershed Committee and would work under the direct supervision of the President of Watershed Committee. He should be selected on the basis of merit and experience.

The honorarium to be paid to the Secretary Watershed shall be charged from the administrative support to the PIA. The Secretary will be responsible for the following tasks:

(a) Convening meetings of the Gram Sabha, Gram Panchayat, Watershed Committee for facilitating the decision-making processes in the context of Watershed Development Projects.
(b) Taking follow-up action on all decisions.
(c) Maintaining all the records of project activities and proceeding of the meetings of the Gram Panchayat, Watershed Committee and other institutions for watershed development project.
(d) Ensuring payments and other financial transactions.
(e) Signing the cheques jointly with the WDT nominee on behalf of the Watershed Committee.

(v) Role of Gram Panchayats (GPs): The Gram Panchayat would perform the following important functions:

(a) Supervise, support and advise Watershed Committee from time to time.
(b) Authenticate the accounts/expenditure statement of Watershed Committee and other institutions of watershed project.
(c) Facilitate the convergence of various projects/schemes to institutions of watershed development projects.
(d) Maintain asset registers under watershed development with a view to retain it after watershed development project.
(e) Allocate usufruct rights to deserving user groups/SHGs over the assets created.

Criteria for Selection of Watershed Projects

The following criteria may broadly be used in selection and prioritization of watershed development projects:

(a) Acuteness of drinking water scarcity.
(b) Extent of overexploitation of groundwater resources.
(c) Preponderance of wastelands/degraded lands.
(d) Contiguity to another watershed that has already been developed/ treated.
(e) Willing of the village community to make voluntary contributions, enforce equitable social regulations for sharing of common property resources, make equitable distribution of benefits,

make arrangements for the operation and maintenance of assets created.

(f) Proportion of SC/STs.

(g) Productivity potential of the land.

(h) Area of the project should not be covered under assured irrigation.

Project Management

The major activities of the watershed development project have been divided into (i) Preparatory, (ii) Works, and (iii) Consolidation and Withdrawal Phase. The total project period may be in the range of four to seven years depending upon the activities of Ministries/Departments. The preparatory phase may be of the duration from 1-2 years. The works phase may be of 2-3 years duration and the third phase of consolidation and withdrawal phase may be of 1-2 years duration.

Preparatory Phase

The major objective of this phase is to build appropriate mechanism for adoption of participatory approach and empowerment of local institutions (WC, SHG and UG). WDT will assume a facilitating role during this phase. The main activities during this phase include:

(a) Taking up entry point activities to establish credibility of the Watershed Development Team (WDT) and create a rapport with the village community. The entry point activities include:

   (i) Works based on urgent needs of the local community such as revival common natural resources, drinking water, development of local energy potential, augmenting ground water potential, etc.

   (ii) Repair, restoration and upgradation of existing common property assets and structures may be undertaken to obtain optimal and sustained benefits from the previous public investments and traditional water harvesting structures.

   (iii) Productivity enhancement of existing farming system could also be an activity that helps in community mobilization and building rapport.

(b) Initiating development of village level institutions such as Watershed Committees (WCs), Self-Help Groups (SHGs) and User Groups (UGs) and capacity-building of different stakeholders on institutional and work related aspects.

(c) Environment building, awareness generation, undertaking of intensive IEC activities, creating involvement and participatory responses.

(d) Baseline survey needed for preparation of Detailed Project Report (DPR), selection of sites and beneficiaries. Every effort must be made to collect gender-disaggregated data to adequately reflect the situation and priorities of woman.

(e) Hydro-geological survey of the watershed to map out zones of potential groundwater recharge, storage and sustainable ground-water utilization.

(f) Building up a network of technical support agencies.

(g) Preparation of DPR, including activities to be carried out, selection of beneficiaries and work sites and design and costing of all works, ensuring that the interests, perceptions and priorities of women, *dalits* and *adivasis* and the landless are adequately reflected in the DPR.

(h) Working out detailed resource use agreement among user group members in a participatory manner based on the principle of equity and sustainability.

(i) Participatory monitoring of progress and processes.

The Watershed Works Phase

This phase is the heart of the programme in which the Detailed Project Report will be implemented. Some of the important activities to be included in this phase are:

(a) *Ridge Area Treatment* — All activities required to restore the health of the catchment area by reducing the volume and velocity surface run-off, including regeneration of vegetative cover in forest and common land, afforestation and staggered trenching, counter and graded bunding, bench terracing, etc.

(b) Drainage line treatment with a combination of vegetative and engineering structures, such as earthen check, brushed checks, gully plugs, loose boulder checks, gabion structures, under-ground dykes, etc.

(c) Development of water harvesting structures such as low cost farm ponds, *nalla* bunds, check dams, percolation tanks and groundwater recharge through wells, bore-wells and other measures.

(d) Nursery raising for fodder, fuel, timber and horticultural species. As far as possible local species may be given priority.

(e) Land Development including *in-situ* soil and moisture conservation and drainage management like field bunds, contour and graded bunds fortified with plantation, bench terracing in hilly terrain, etc.
(f) Crop demonstration for popularizing new crops/varieties, water saving technologies such as drip irrigation or innovative management practices. As far as possible varieties based on the local germplasm may be promoted.
(g) Pasture development, sericulture, bee keeping, backward poultry, small ruminant, other livestock and micro-enterprises.
(h) Veterinary services for livestock and other livestock improvement measures.
(i) Fisheries development in village ponds/tanks, farm, ponds, etc.
(j) Promotion and propagation of non-conventional energy saving devices, energy consumption measures, biofuel plantations, etc.

Consolidation and Withdrawal Phase

In this phase the resources augmented and economic plans developed in phase II are made the foundation to create new nature based, sustainable livelihoods and raise productivity levels.

The main objectives of this phase are:

(a) Consolidation and completion of various works.
(b) Building the capacity of the community based organizations to carry-out the new agenda items during post-project period.
(c) Sustainable management of (developed) natural resources.
(d) Upscaling of successful experiences regarding farm production systems/off-farm livelihoods.

An indicative list of various activities during this phase is given below:

1. *Consolidation of various works:*

   (a) Preparation of the project completion report with details about status of each interventions.
   (b) Documentation of successful experiences as well as lessons learnt for future use.

2. *Management of developed natural resources:*

   (a) Improving the sustainability of various interventions under the project.

(b) Formal allocation of user rights over Common Property Resources (CPRs).
(c) Collection of user charges for CPRs.
(d) Repair, maintenance and protection of CPRs.
(e) Sustainable utilization of developed natural resources.
(f) Involvement of Gram Panchayat/corresponding institutions (as a governance body) in addressing the above aspects.

3. *Intensification of farm production system/off-farm livelihoods:*

(a) Upscaling of successful experiences related to above aspects through revolving fund under the project as well as credit and technical support from external institutions.
(b) Promotion of agro-processing, marketing arrangements of produce and similar off-farm and informal sector enterprises.
(c) Farmers may also be encouraged to develop non-pesticidal management, low cost organic inputs, seed farms and links with wider markets to fetch competitive price.

4. *Project management related aspects:*

(a) Participatory planning, implementation and monitoring of activities to be carried out during consolidation phase.
(b) Terminal evaluation of project as per the executed outcomes.

The implementation of new common guidelines for watershed development projects issued in 2008 (and reissued with minor modifications in 2011) required a major change in the mode of implementation of the programme. However, in a comprehensive review programme carried out in 2012, it emerged that a number of practical impediments were coming in the way of putting the new paradigm of watershed management into practice on the ground and pace of the programme was found to be less than satisfactory. It was also felt that the role of NRAA *vis-à-vis* the department of land resources needed clear demarcation. In June 2012, the Ministry of Rural Development constituted a committee under the Chairmanship of Dr. Mihir Shah, member of Planning Commission to revisit the common guidelines for watershed development projects to provide necessary flexibility within the guidelines and to ensure momentum to the IWMP, even while strengthening its innovative features.

Innovative Features of the 2012 guidelines

The new guidelines have been formulated by the Mihir Shah Committee after extensive consultation with the states and the relevant stakeholders. They strengthen the innovative features of the earlier guidelines but also make certain changes to impart greater flexibility, clarity and momentum to IWMP. The key features of the new guidelines are summarized as follows:

(a) *Duration:* In order to provide greater momentum to the programme and avoid thin spreading of resources, it has been decided to make the IWMP a five year programme.

(b) *Professionalism:* One of the key deficiencies of programme was found to be the shortage of funds to deploy high quality professional human resources for both social and technical aspects. Hence, a special allocation of 10 per cent of the total project cost has been proposed for deployment of professional human resources.

(c) *Capacity-building:* A new national strategy for capacity-building has been unveiled, since this was a key requirement of the programme that needed much greater direction and momentum.

(d) *Institution-building:* This crucial element required to ensure sustainability of benefits under the programme continues to be neglected. Hence, a special provision has been made for this crucial activity and guidelines issued to facilitate the same.

(e) *Role of Civil Society:* Various reviews of the watershed programme show that some of the best work has been done by civil society organizations. The new guideline seek to provide further scope and facilitation for civil society participation in the programme, even while proposing a new and transparent procedure for their selection.

(f) *Ridge to Valley Approach:* A watershed programme must follow the ridge to valley approach since the ridge is the catchment of streams and water bodies in the lower reaches. If these catchments are treated, the capacities of the dams in the valley are likely to be impaired. However, it is also to be recognized that this is a participatory programme that needs buy-in from the community. Hence, some work may initially be done in the lower reaches near the village settlements so that the people can understand the benefits of the programme and feel a ownership over it. However, in each case, it must be ensured that the ridges/catchments of each water body are treated fully soon thereafter.

(g) *Size of Watershed:* Experience has shown that both from the point of view of economies of scale and proper planning, the ideal size of a watershed project should be between 3,000-7,000 hectares. Wherever possible, additional watersheds in contiguous areas may be taken up so as to form larger clusters. However, smaller size projects may be sanctioned in hilly/ difficult terrain areas.

(h) *Higher Unit Cost:* Given the rate of inflation since the per hectare unit cost of ₹ 15,000 per hectare for normal areas and ₹ 18,000 per hectare for special areas (desert, hilly and IAP districts).

(i) *Smoother Fund Release Procedure:* To overcome the avoidable in the progress of work, a new set of expeditious fund release procedure are outlined in these guidelines.

(j) *Setting Up a Central Level Nodal Agency (CLNA):* Many states have expressed the need for more intensive support from the centre. A strong professionally managed CLNA is to be set up with major facilitating responsibilities elaborated in these guidelines. The role of NRAA is also being suitably redefined in line with the recommendations of the working group for the Twelfth Five Year Plan so that the synergy and complimentarity between CLNA and NRAA can provide requisite support to the watershed programme.

(k) *Work on Forest Land:* A major concern emerging especially in tribal areas has been the procedural complexities of work in ridge areas that fall within forest lands. The new guideline offer a framework within which this work can be facilitated.

(l) *Focus on Physical Outcomes and Monitorable Indicators:* This guideline provide a clear list of monitorable indicators and green metrics that will be tracked on a regular basis to ensure that the massive outlets are converted into enduring outcomes on the ground.

3

REVIEW OF LITERATURE

The watershed development programmes in the country are undertaken with multiple objectives ranging from rehabilitation of degraded areas to conservation of the resource base and improvement in the productivity of agriculture. It aims at mitigating adverse impacts of drought and resource degradation which will contribute to reduction in production risk and protecting livelihoods. Conservation of the resource base will contribute to sustainable productivity growth in agriculture. In recent years, the watershed development programmes have increasingly focused on poverty. Enhancing people's livelihoods, reduction in poverty and sustainability are increasingly recognized as being the main objectives of watershed programmes. There have been many studies done by various individuals and institutions to assess the impacts of projects on the ecology and economy of that particular area. A large number of studies have approved the WDPs in terms of its benefits on the productivity, employment opportunity and ecological impacts. An attempt has been made here to briefly review these studies.

In many cases, the benefits from watershed projects may not have also been equitably distributed to benefit the poorest of the poor. In some of the cases, the poor actually become worse off, because the measures for soil and water conservation have restricted their access to common resources (Kerr *et al.*, 2000). Failing to account for the needs of the poor not only makes watershed development less effective in reaching one of its main goals, but also affects sustainability of the overall outcomes. If the poor are unable to maintain or enhance their livelihood through access to existing or new benefit schemes, the tendency will increase for common property resource management arrangements to breakdown. The NGOs perform better than the government managed projects because of mainly two factors, i.e. scale of operation and staffing time. While the government projects have huge budgets and work in hundreds of villages, the NGOs mostly work in a limited number of villages. The community organization part in the NGOs is better than the government sector. While the Government people are more concerned only with the watershed projects, the NGOs devote a lot of time for the social organization.

Rosegrant *et al.*, (2002) in their cross-country study concluded that "the water harvesting has the potential in some regions to improve rainfed crop yields, and can provide farmers with improved water availability and increased soil fertility in some local and regional eco-systems, as well as environmental benefits through reduced soil erosion. However, despite localized successes, broader farmer acceptance of water harvesting techniques has been limited, due to the high cost of implementation and higher short-term risk due to the necessity of additional inputs, cash and labour. Water harvesting initiatives frequently suffer from lack of hydrological data and insufficient attention during the planning stages to important social and economic considerations and the absence of a long-term government strategy for ensuring sustainability of interventions." The authors noted that the greater involvement of farmers for planning and maintenance and provision of appropriate educational and extension support helped in expanding the contribution of water harvesting methods.

ICRISAT and the National Agriculture Research System (NARS) in Asia have developed in partnership an innovative and upscalable consortium model for managing watershed holistically. In this approach, rainwater management is used as an entry point activity starting with the *in-situ* conservation of rainwater and converging the benefits of stored rainwater into increased productivity by using improved crops, cultivars, suitable nutrient and pest management practices and land and water management practices (S.P. Wani *et al.*, 2009). The Integrated Genetic Natural Resource Management (IGNRM) approach has enabled communities not only to harness the benefits of watershed management but also to achieve much of the potential from improved varieties from a wider range of crops. The household incomes and overall productivity have more than doubled. The benefits accrue not only to landholding households but also to the landless marginalized groups through the creation of greater employment opportunities. The share of crops in household income during the drought year in 2002 declined from 44 per cent to 12 per cent in the non-project villages, the crop income largely remained unchanged from 36 per cent to 37 per cent in the watershed village during the same year. The loss in the household income in non-project villages was largely compensated by migration and non-farm income which increased from 49 per cent in an average year to 75 per cent during the drought year in 2002. Much of this gain originates from improved soil fertility management and increased soil availability of irrigation water and integration of improved cultivars and cropping patterns into the watershed systems.

Dr. Wani stated "While the INRM approach has made significant contributions in re-orienting research for sustainable management of natural resources, there is now a need to create clear synergies with germplasm improvement and the income and livelihood strategies of resource users. The IGNRM approaches espoused by ICRISAT with projects that pursue the IGNRM approach (e.g. integrated management of community watersheds) provide optimism about the effectiveness and suitability of this approach".

In an analysis of the state level Comprehensive Watershed Development Programme (COWDEP) of Maharashtra, significant changes in the household economy were observed (Deshpande and Reddy, 1991). The study covers 30 blocks in the State and indicated concentration of certain specific components and overall good results of technology. It was observed that the employment generated in each of the watershed was 30,000 man days depending on the various agro-climatic zones of the location. In the study area, the crop pattern, crop intensity, proportion of wasteland and yield per hectare has changed substantially. The yield levels of paddy, *ragi*, pulses, *bajra*, wheat, sun flower rises by 18, 34, 7, 46, 11 and 64 per cent respectively, whereas the yield level of *jowar* decreases by 2 per cent. Moisture availability has increased in the watershed regions. The study also made a comparative analysis of the cases of active beneficiary participation against passive participation. Singh *et al.*, (1991) reported that due to the implementation of watershed development programmes in Karnataka, the net income from all the crops increased to ₹ 1,970/ha area from ₹ 1,456/ha. The authors reviewed various activities like forestry, animal husbandry, soil conservation and horticultural activities of Punjab. The Benefit-Cost ratio of the above activities worked out to be 2.74, 1.14 and 7.05 respectively. The benefit-cost ratio for all the component of the project is 0.95. Due to horticultural activities, the net income rises within the range of ₹ 825 to ₹ 2,780.

P.K. Joshi *et al.* (2007) analyzed the performance of 311 watersheds in India. In this analysis, he revealed that watershed programmes are silently revolutionalizing rainfed areas, with positive impacts with the benefit-cost ratio of 2.46 in low income regions as compared to 1.98 in high income regions. The employment generation was 175 days and 132 days for low income and high income regions respectively. In the study Joshi *et al.*, opined that the success of the watershed depends on the involvement of the stakeholders in the planning and implementation of the project. The study has documented and analyzed the benefits from various watershed projects. It emphasized on the fact that a programme will never succeed unless it is economically viable and therefore economic efficiencies of watershed programmes were also documented and analyzed. It is observed that the watershed programmes have been effective in augmenting water resources along with conservation of soil and water in the rainfed areas. In addition watershed programmes have also generated considerable income and employment in the fragile rainfed areas.

Farrington *et al.* (1999) also provided an overview of the recorded impact of watershed development programmes in the country. Results indicate that successful projects in fact have reduced rainwater run-off and recharge groundwater and surface water aquifers, improved drinking water supply, increased the irrigation area, changed cropping patterns, crop intensity and agricultural productivity, increased availability of fuel and fodder, improved soil fertility and changed the composition of livestock. The impact of these projects on poverty alleviation and long-term sustainability of project results were however less clear. Although some projects did seem to have paid attention to the needs of the landless and poor, their impact on poverty reduction was not assessed.

B.K. Panda *et al.* (2006) collected data from 200 households of Kashipur block of Rayagada district of Odisha. In their analysis, it was observed that due to irrigation potential of the watershed development projects in dryland areas, there has been positive change on cropping pattern by means of crop shifting from traditional crops to more valuable cash crops. Perceptible changes are noticed in the yield rate of almost all the crops and gross return per hectare of land is found satisfactory. It has been observed that though the overall impact of watershed programmes is encouraging, still there is very large-scale food insecurity to the extent of 84 per cent in the watershed area. The productivity of various crops has increased to a marked extent but the cropping intensity has not changed much because the cropping activities are confined only to the *kharif* and not sustainable during the *rabi* season. The change in gross return per hectare is more than 200 per cent for all cereals. In *the analysis* there has been a comparison between the project and non-project area of the same block. The Yield rate of various crops in the project area are much higher than the non-project area of the Kashipur block.

Abraham Samuel *et al.* (2007) evaluated a sample of 405 micro-watersheds, of Maharashtra comprising of around 4 per cent of the completed projects in the state, covering 20 districts and all five regions of the State. The study looked into the bio-physical impacts such as erosion control and soil moisture improvement. The improvement in the bio-physical aspects like the soil and moisture conservation is reported by around 47 per cent of the watersheds. Groundwater improvement is reported in a large number of watersheds (69%), almost three-fourth of watershed report the increase in the irrigation potential. It finds that the overall watershed strategy has realized a lot of its potential in a large number of its projects in terms of the improvement in bio-physical resource base.

Sibranjan Mishra (1991), in his Micro study of a watershed project in West Bengal, observed that watershed approach significantly increased the productivity of the farm and labour employment and also fuel resources. Ganesh Pangare (1992) and his team made an experiment on people's participation in Ralegaon Sidhi region. It was a drought-prone area but after the implementation of the watershed projects in the area, it is now a green village and has attained sustainability through proper harvesting and resource management techniques.

Surya Vanshi and Patil (1991) studied the economic impact of the Kalhewadi Project. They found that the development activities have taken through soil and water conservation measures such as the construction of percolation tanks, farm ponds, contour bunding, etc. After the implementation of the project, the number of effective wells increased from 34 to 74 and thus water level has increased from 3.5 mts. to 6.85 mts in this region. The major results of the project are (i) water use increased from 430 cm to 2,232 cm and employment generation has increased over the period of the scheme.

Sidhu *et. al.* (1991) studied watershed management in an area where assured irrigation facilities are lacking, canal irrigation is very limited and the installation of tubewell is very expensive. Under such situations they suggest watershed projects for the development of the area. They have selected three different areas for the implementation of the project. Of these three areas, two have proved to be economically viable and significantly enhanced the productivity of the beneficiaries in the command area.

U.S. Patnaik *et al.* (2004) studied the impact of Kokriguda Watershed Project and found that due to watershed in the tribal dominated village there has been a perceptible crop diversification and increase in the productivity of land. The number of vegetable growers increased from 5 to 33 in a span of 5 years and there is also a fourfold increase in the gross area under vegetable cultivation. The vegetable cultivation in the watershed generated employment potential of 3,762 number of man days/annum, which discouraged the male outmigration to the nearby towns. Net results obtained from vegetables were ₹ 15,625 per farmer and ₹ 14,245 per ha. Improvement in the standard of the living of the villagers was observed. The benefit-cost ratio of Kokriguda watershed was worked out to be 1.65 and 1.89 for arable and non-arable lands respectively. It is also reported that due to the watershed projects there were some intangible benefits like attitudinal change, clothing and food habit, cleanliness, increase in awareness and empowerment, increased access to development agencies.

User participation is increasingly being recognized as critical for success in watershed development and management projects (Nancy Johnson *et al.*, 2001). Local residents were not considered in the formulation of top down watershed projects, resulting in plans and technologies that were inconsistent with people's needs and ignorant of local people's vast and detailed knowledge of land and land use practices. Empirical evidence suggests that giving users a role in managing their own watershed resources can lead to projects that are more efficient and effective than their top down predecessors. User participation also has implications for watershed management research. In addition to changing the way technologies and practices are developed and disseminated, participation broadens the research agenda, bringing in new topics like organizational behaviour, collective action and conflict resolution.

John Kerr *et al.* (2002) in a detailed survey of Maharashtra and Andhra Pradesh States, covering 86 villages to evaluate the performance of watershed development projects compares conditions in the study villages before and after the projects were implemented. Quantitative analysis at the village level examines performance indicators such as change in access to irrigation water, employment opportunity, soil erosion and conservation on uncultivated lands and drainage lines, and availability of various products such as fodder from the common lands. At the plot level, performance indicators include changes in cropping intensity, yields and soil erosion on cultivated lands, farmers' land investments and net returns to cultivation. It was observed that in both Maharashtra and Andhra Pradesh, the participatory projects performed better than their technocratic, top-down counterparts. However, participation combined with sound technical input performed best for all.

Regarding equity aspect in the projects Kerr *et al.* (2002) mentioned "Problems remain regarding equity. By their nature area development programmes offer benefits primarily to landowners, with landless people benefitting indirectly, either through peripheral programme activities or trickle down effects. In fact watershed projects can actually make women and landless people worse off by restricting their access to resources that contribute to their livelihoods. Even some of the more participatory have found it difficult to ensure that benefits reach all of the intended population: respondents perceived that projects benefit rose with land-holding size, and landless and near landless people were most likely to report negative effects from the projects. The very best projects help the poorest and the politically weakest community members negotiate with their neighbours to ensure that everyone benefits, but this remains an area where nearly all projects need to improve".

The traditional natural resources use in the rural communities has significantly evolved over the years. In the past, priority of watershed management was given to the biophysical framework of watershed which is often based on top-down approach (Rhoades and Elliot, 2000). However, in the traditional system, local people were often not consulted in the design of top-down approach, which resulted in failure in projects in achieving the project goals. Watershed projects are more efficient and effective when users are given a role in managing their own watershed resources (Johnson *et al.*, 2001).

Several useful studies have been conducted to assess the contribution of participatory watershed programmes (Turton *et al.*, 1998, Kerr *et al.*, 20002, Wani *et al.*, 2005, Joshi *et al.*, 2003 and Reddy *et al.*, 2004) and the results from these studies are discussed below.

Many studies revealed that participatory watershed projects had a positive impact on crop productivity. Due to the increased irrigated area under watershed area helped in the crop productivity (Shah, 2001). Productivity gains were reported to be greater in case of rainfed crops. Average yields of rainfed crops (e.g. soybean and legumes) increased by as much as 280 per cent (Renfro, 2005). This information suggest that participatory watershed management programmes made significant impact in terms of the productivity gains in rainfed areas which contributes to increased farm income and better livelihoods of the poor in fragile and high risk environment. The watershed programmes have also helped in soil moisture content. Many farmers in the watershed development area reported an increase in soil moisture level (Shah, 2001). This improved soil moisture will open new opportunities for diversifying farming activities in rainfed areas. Due to the watershed programmes cropping intensity will be increased significantly and it is observed that cropping intensity is increased by 13-25 per cent (Renfro, 2005).

Soil and water conservation measures adopted in the watershed development projects were helpful in augmenting water storage capacity and improving local water resources by reducing the rate of run-off and increasing the groundwater recharge (Butterworth *et al.*, 2001).

Bekele Shiferaw *et al.* (2008) using empirical data from 87 watershed communities in the semi-arid India has shown that collective action in watershed management can be captured through as set of variables that indicate the capacity of the communities to design and enforce certain common institutional arrangements, and their ability to mobilize local financial and labour resources for watershed investments. The overall results indicate that collective action has made a significant contribution in terms of improving the investments and management of critical jointly held natural resource assets (such as wells, check dams, community forest, grazing land, etc.) but there is a lack of evidence on its effects on improving the assets endowments of the resource poor and reducing poverty level within the semi-arid watershed villages included in the study.

In the Meta analysis of 311 watershed case studies in India (Wani *et al.*, 2005), it has been revealed that watershed programmes are silently revolutionalizing rainfed areas with positive impacts. It has been calculated that the benefit-cost ratio of 1 : 2.14, internal rate of return of 22 per cent, cropping intensity increased by 63 per cent, irrigated area increased by 34 per cent, run-off reduction by 13 per cent and employment increased 181 persons man days/year/ha. Based on detailed studies and synthesis of the results, impacts, shortcomings and knowledge gained from a large number of watershed programmes and on farm experiences, an ICRISAT-led consortium is an innovative farmer participatory consortium model for watershed management. The ICRISAT model ensured improved productivity with the adoption of cost efficient water harvesting structures (WHS) as an entry point for improving livelihoods. The integrated watershed management deals with conservation and efficient use of rainwater, groundwater, land and other natural resources for increasing agricultural productivity and improving livelihoods.

S.P. Wani *et al.*, with the support of International Crop Research Institute for the Semi Arid Tropics (ICRISAT) has developed a novel model to address the issue of the efficient use of natural resources in rainfed areas. The Natural Resource Management (NRM) team at ICRISAT led by Dr. S.P. Wani adopted the participatory consortium model which is a unique model extended to their flagship watershed management project. This model has been adopted with great success in one of the ICRISAT's watershed projects at Kothapally village of Andhra Pradesh in India. This model was an innovative model with a consortium of institutions was formed for the project implementation. In this approach, all the government authorities were involved in the consortium from the beginning. Participation of local community was central to this approach and community participation will be encouraged by various communities. The important element of the model was using 'user pay' principle without giving any subsidies for investments on individual's farm for technologies, input and conservation measures.

Impact of consortium watershed model:

- Sustainable increase in productivity of crops.
- Intensive avenue plantation has come up in wastelands of the project area.
- Significant reduction in run-off and soil loss.
- Groundwater levels were improved and additional lands were irrigated with additional groundwater recharge.
- Crop productivity was optimized by adopting integrated water, crop and nutrient management in the watershed.
- Vegetation cover was increased from 129 ha to 200 ha.
- With improved technologies farmers obtained high crop yields, particularly in drylands.
- Net returns on rainfed cereal crops have more than doubled.
- Watershed projects contributed towards capacity development of the local people.
- The consortium model also contributed towards the poverty reduction by increasing average household income.

M.K. Rathod (2008), emphasized the impact of watershed development programmes on the Korku tribe in Melghat in Maharashtra and Madhya Pradesh those who are dependent on the agriculture and forest for their livelihood. He evaluated the effectiveness of watershed development programme on personal, socio-economic and situational profiles of the Korku farmers and adoption behaviour about soil and water conservation practices and relationships. It has been observed that the cropping intensity of the tribals of the study area has increased substantially due to the contact of the external personnel with the tribals.

Some of major constraints in the adoption of soil and water conservation practices by the Korku tribe are that of lack of knowledge, non-availability of manpower at proper time and traditional agriculture. These farmers have recorded an overall increase of 53.77 per cent in agricultural productivity. The per capita income of the respondents was ₹ 3,649.55 before the project which increased to ₹ 5,508.65 after the project. The cropping intensity of the tribal farmers too increased to a substantial figure.

R. Mani (2006), studied the impact of watershed development projects on the employment generation on the people of South Arcot district of Tamil Nadu. In his analysis, it is found that additional employment opportunity in primary sector is 27,292 which is generated through crop diversification, expansion of area under cultivation, soil conservation, minor irrigation, percolation pond, inter-cropping, afforestation, agro-forestry, social forestry, animal husbandry and dairy unit. In the secondary sector, the employment generation of 891 have been worked out through the development of agro-based, mineral based and service oriented industries, tannery work and leather collection units. In the tertiary sector 4,256 numbers of additional employment opportunities have been worked out through area oriented, skill oriented, scheme oriented, sector oriented, group oriented and other programmes.

Reddy *et al.* (2001), evaluated some of the successful watershed development projects of Andhra Pradesh implemented under the Common Guidelines of 1994 found that in the sample area the inequalities among the poor and rich have declined after the implementation of the watershed projects. They have emphasized on the role of participation of the community in the planning and implementation for the success of these projects. The selection of programme implementing agencies is important for the greater sustainability and efficiency of the project.

There have been studies which show that the watershed development approach has been more successful than the poverty alleviation and employment generation programmes like the JRY, NREP and NFFWP. The watershed development programmes are designed to create both employment and assets for the local people, taking advantage of the natural capacity for regeneration inherent in a biomass based system (Chopra and Kadekoli, 1993). A study of the Kandi Watershed Development Programme by Singh *et al.* (1993) found that in case of the families engaged in the agriculture, the income inequality has widened. From the sample study, it is found that the Gini coefficient ratio for household income increased from 0.32 in 1979-80 to 0.42 in

1986-87. The large farmers take better advantage of the projects than the smaller counterparts in productivity of various crops.

Soussan and Reddy (2003) in an analysis of expenditure pattern shows that more than 70 per cent funds are used for land and water management interventions that predominantly benefit larger farmers and only 7.5 per cent are being used support the livelihoods to the poor and landless families. In their analysis, it is observed that the income gap between the rich and poor farmers is increasing through these projects which are a matter of great concern for the development planners.

In the study covering 36 projects across five states Kolavalli and Kerr (2002) highlighted the fact that except for a few NGO and NGO-Government collaborative projects, community participation is relatively insignificant. Majority of the decisions are being taken by the PIAs before the implementation of the project. In the study it was emphasized that the higher levels of participation are associated with beneficiary contribution. People's contribution or cost sharing in watershed management is another commonly used indicator of participation. The cost sharing is supposed to enhance participation and it also serves as an indirect indicator that people have been part of the decision-making process. Maintenance of conservation measures has been found to be positively associated with the share of the cost borne by the community members. Kerr and Kolavalli (2002) highlighted three important dimensions of participation, which relates to group participation. These are: (i) facilitating collective action, (ii) transferring critical decision making powers, and (iii) making communities share the development costs and benefits with the implementing organizations, therefore, need to play the important role of fostering and increasing the overall level of community participation in the planning and development of watersheds.

In the mid-term appraisal of the Ninth Plan of the Planning Commission articulated satisfactory and unsatisfactory performance of watershed programmes on different dimensions (Government of India, 2001c). On a satisfactory note it states that beneficial impacts such as increase in cropping intensity, change in cropping patterns, increase in crop productivity and increase in underground water recharge as a result of the conservation measures, reduction in soil and run-off losses with lesser siltation effect and reduction in sedimentation at the watershed level. These projects have also generated employment and increased family income through diversified farming system such as livestock development, dryland horticulture and household production activities. On the other side it stated that the increase in agricultural production did not last for more than two years. Structures were abandoned because of the lack of maintenance and there was no mechanism for looking after the common lands. Many projects have failed to generate sustainability because of the failure of the government agencies to involve people.

Kundan Kumar *et al.* (2001), in their report on the Tenure and Access rights as constraints to community watershed development in Odisha studied the complex dynamics of shifting cultivation and *jholas* in the study area of undivided Koraput district. The land and forest of the tribal areas are inadequately captured by the formal land and forest tenure system, creating ambiguities and conflicts with bearing on both livelihoods and sustainability. In its study, they observed that the disjunctions between the actual land use and the legal categorization of the land have major implications on livelihoods and development in the area, including WDPs. Some of the important externalities in the watershed development are created because of these disjunctions. On the generation of externalities in the sample watersheds it is observed that externalities are linked to heterogeneity of property rights and linkages between downstream and upstream users. For the above purpose seven case studies from the undivided Koraput district were taken and it was suggested that the initial entry point activity and survey should include a 'rights regime' survey in the watershed in which the official and informal rights and tenure situation should be mapped out and usufruct rights should be given to the people in order to make the shifting cultivation unattractive. Training and capacity-building programmes should be taken up to help the watershed development team members become familiar with the land and forest tenure issues.

Santosh Kumar Sahu (2006) in the cost-benefit analysis of watershed management projects has taken two watersheds one each from Odisha and Rajasthan as sample for the analysis of the impact and cost-benefit ratio of both the projects. The sample size taken for the analysis is 100 households each from Odisha and Rajasthan. One watershed each from Kashipur block of Odisha and Bichiwada district of Rajasthan has been taken for sample study. In his findings he is of the opinion that the stakeholders of the projects in Odisha and Rajasthan have been benefited in terms of the agricultural productivity, wage earnings and income from the livestock. It was observed by him that the benefit cost ratio in Odisha project is marginally higher than the Rajasthan project. But it was found that the investment in Rajasthan project could be more cost beneficial than its Odisha counterpart. It was calculated that the per capita benefit is ₹ 1,014.45 in Rajasthan as compared to ₹ 847.00 in

Odisha Project. The overall benefit in case of the project implemented by the NGO Seva Mandir in the case of the Rajasthan is better than the Kashipur Project of Odisha which is managed by the Government department.

Watershed development projects have greater potential to generate employment opportunities to the rural people. This was due to the increased availability of water resources, diversified cropping pattern including cultivation of labour intensive vegetable crops and other horticultural crops (Reddy *et al.*, 2001). This additional employment generation from a watershed programme varies across regions depending on the cropping intensity, and labour intensive crops grown in that region. The additional employment generation in the villages led to minimizing migration of landless and other labour. Thus, watershed programmes also contributed towards checking migration of rural people to the urban areas. This migration has greater concern for planning and devising rural development strategies.

The role and importance of community participation in ensuring the success and sustainability of watershed management is now widely accepted. In order to maximize the efficiency of exterior aid the managers and owners of the individual and common lands must be involved from the outset. The first hand knowledge of their environment coupled with their local technologies are indispensable elements in the success of a watershed management project. Since, the impact of the activities is felt by the entire community, it is clearly in the interest of the project that the divergent groups of the community be mobilized and motivated. These groups must include the landless generally women and other weaker social groups in order to balance the powerful influence of certain individuals and families on the community decision (S. Chatterji, 2002).

Aparna Kanungo (2002) studied the Kattery watershed under Indo-German Bilateral Project (IGBP) in the threshold of Ooty town of Tamil Nadu in which both the Government agencies and the non-governmental organizations work together. Some of the important findings by the author in the above project are:

- All the three partners the State Government department, the NGO and the community should be involved right from the initial phase of the project. It is, therefore, imperative that the NGO should be given lead time of at least six months so that they can motivate and create awareness within the community about the programme.

- For ensuring sustainability, it is important that the community be involved in all stages of project implementation, i.e. planning, execution and follow-up management.
- Since, the entire community would feel the impact, it is, therefore, necessary to involve and mobilize the different class and caste groups within the community. Special emphasis should be given to the needs of women and particularly the poor and disadvantaged sections of the society.
- It is desirable that the selected NGO should have some experience in the project area.
- For effective collaboration, it is important that both partners should have mutual respect for each other. Regular meetings should be held between two partners to have to review the progress of the ongoing activities.

It has been noted that participatory watershed management projects have been raising income, agricultural productivity, generating employment and conserving soil and water resources (Yoganand *et al.*, 2006). Evidence from the field study by many researchers suggest that watershed development brought several positive trends including diversification of rural economy, development of new institutions, increasing cropping intensity, improved fodder production, increased availability of drinking water with rising groundwater table, capacity development of the community, etc. Based on the evidence from various studies, it has been suggested that participatory watershed management could be a viable strategy of rural development for achieving sustainable rural livelihoods in India.

The review of literature on watershed development programmes reveals that there have been many studies on impact assessment of these projects in various parts of the country. Most of the studies are confined to the western and southern States of India and very limited work has been done on the projects of Odisha in general and a backward district like Koraput in particular. The district of Koraput in Odisha is one of the most backward regions in the country. Therefore, the present study is intended to study the impact of WDPs, which is one of the flagship programmes of the government for the holistic and sustainable development, on the underprivileged sections of the society like the ST and SC population of the area.

The present study proposes to evaluate the performance of the already completed watershed projects in the district. The objectives of this study are to evaluate the impact of the projects on the economy and ecology of the area in the pre- and post-project period. Against this background, the objectives of the study are set. The detailed objectives and hypothesis of the study are mentioned in Chapter 1.

4

WATERSHED DEVELOPMENT PROGRAMMES
A Profile of the Study Area

State Profile

Odisha lies on the east coast of India. It is surrounded by West Bengal on the north-east, Bihar on the north, Andhra Pradesh on the south-east, Chhattisgarh on the west and Bay of Bengal on the east. The whole state lies in the tropical zone and is divided into four distinct tracts, *viz.* the northern plateau, the Eastern Ghats, the central tract and coastal plains. The State is drained by three great rivers — the Mahanadi, the Brahmani, the Baitarni — and some small rivers which flow into the Bay of Bengal. Odisha comprises 4.74 per cent of the country's land mass. It has 36.80 million people comprising 3.58 per cent of the population of the country (Census, 2001). Nearly 85 per cent of the population live in rural areas and they depend mostly on agriculture for their livelihood. The State has abundant mineral resources including precious and semi-precious stones. It has also plentiful water resources. According to the estimates of the Central Ground Water Board, the total groundwater resources in Odisha was 21.011 billion cubic metres (BCM) in 2001, out of which 60 per cent, i.e. 12.607 BCM is safe and usable. The gross annual draft for all uses in 2001 was 3.011 billion cubic metre (BCM). Accordingly, 14.79 per cent groundwater resources had been harnessed till 2001. Cultivators and agricultural labourers constitute 65 per cent of the total workforce. Hence, agriculture provides direct or indirect employment to 65 per cent of the total workforce and contributes 26 per cent of the net state domestic product. *Kharif* is the main cropping season and rice is the principal crop during *kharif* season. Cropping during the *Rabi* season is mainly confined to irrigated areas and areas with residual moisture. Other important crops produced in the State are pulses (Arhar, Mung, Kulthi, Biri), Oilseeds (Groundnut, Til, Mustard and Niger), Fibres (Jute, Mesta, Cotton), Sugarcane, Vegetables and Spices. Mango, Banana, Coconut and cashew are the main horticultural crops of the State.

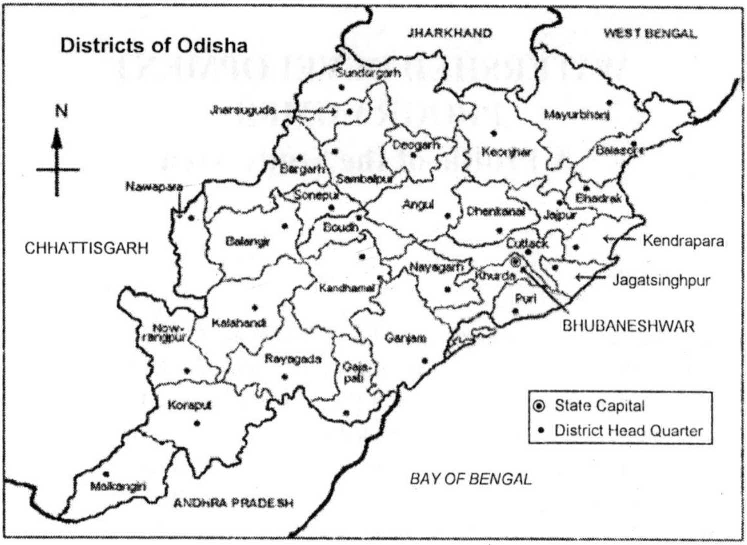

Map 4.1: State of Odisha

The State has cultivated area of 62 lakh hectares out of which 27 lakh hectares is high land, 19 lakh hectares is medium and 16 lakh hectares low land. Paddy occupies about 42 lakh hectares in *Kharif* season and 2.5 lakh hactares during *Rabi* season.

The entire State is divided into ten agro-climatic zones (Table 4.1) on the basis of soil, weather and other relevant characteristics. The agriculture in Odisha is characterized by low productivity due to traditional agricultural practices, inadequate irrigation infrastructure, small size of holding and low investment. The cropping intensity of Odisha was 162 per cent in the year 2008-09, which shows an increasing trend due to the availability of irrigation to more and more areas. The cropping intensity has increased from 135 per cent in 2000-01 to 162 per cent in 2008-09. The cropping intensity is highest in Puri district (214%) followed by Sonepur and Cuttack (197%). The lowest cropping intensity has been recorded in Sundargarh (129%) (*Odisha Economic Survey*, 2009-10, p. 75).

Table 4.1: Agro-climatic Zones in Odisha

Sl: No.	*Agro-climatic Zone*	*Agricultural Districts*	*Climate*	*Mean Annual Rainfall*	*Mean Maximum Temp.*	*Mean Minimum Temp.*	*Broad Soil Groups*
1.	North Western Plateau	Sundargarh, part of Deogarh, Sambalpur, Jharsuguda	Hot, Moist and Sub-humid	1600	38.0	15.0	Red, Brown forest, Red and Yellow, Mixed Red and Black
2.	North Central Plateau	Mayurbhanj, parts of Keonjhar	Hot, Moist and Sub-humid	1534	36.6	11.1	Lateritic, Red and Yellow Mixed Red and Black
3.	North Eastern Costal Plain	Balasore, Bhadrak and parts of Jajpur	Moist Humid	1568	36.0	14.8	Red, Lateritic, Deltaic Alluvial, Costal Alluvial and Waline
4.	East and South Eastern Costal Plain	Kendrapara, Khurda, Jagatsinghpur, Cuttack, Puri, Nayagarh and parts of Ganjam	Hot and Humid	1577	39.0	11.5	Saline, Lateritic, Alluvial Red and Mixed Red and Black
5.	North Eastern Ghat	Phulbani, Rayagada, Gajapati and parts of Ganjam and Koraput	Hot, Moist and Sub-humid	1597	37.0	10.4	Brown Forest, Lateritic, Alluvial, Red, Mixed Red and Black
6.	Eastern Ghat High Land	Major parts of Koraput, Nabarangpur	Warm Humid	1522	34.1	7.5	Red, Mixed Red & Black Mixed Red and Yellow
7.	South Eastern Ghat	Malkangiri and parts of Keonjhar	Warm and Humid	1710	34.1	13.2	Red, Lateritic, Black
8.	Western Undulating Zone	Kalahandi and Nuapada	Hot, Moist and sub-humid	1352	37.8	11.9	Black, Mixed Red and Yellow
9.	Western Central Table Land	Bargarh, Bolangir, Boudh, Sonepur parts of Sambalpur and Jharsuguda	Hot, Moist and Sub-humid	1614	40.0	12.4	Red and Yellow, Red Brown Forest, Lateritic
10.	Mid Central Table Land	Angul, Dhenkanal, parts of Cuttack and Jajpur	Hot, Moist and Sub-humid	1421	38.7		Alluvial, Red, Lateritic, Mixed Red and Black

Source: Department of Agriculture, Government of Odisha.

Water Resources

Odisha depends largely upon monsoon for its water resources. South west monsoon triggers rainfall in the State. About 78 per cent of the total annual rainfall occurs during the period from June to September and the balance 22 per cent in the remaining period. In addition to the seasonal availability, the rainfall in the State also shows spatial variation, i.e. from about 1200 mm in southern coastal plain to about 1,700 mm in northern plateau. The long-term average annual rainfall in the State is of the order 1482 mm. Under normal condition, the State receives annual precipitation of about 230.76 billion cubic metres (BCM) of water. Of the total precipitation, a part is lost by evaporation, transpiration and deep percolation and a part stored in the form of groundwater reserve and the remaining appears as surface run-off. The groundwater reserve and surface run-off constitute the water resources of the State. The water resource scenario of Odisha and India are given in Table 4.2.

Table 4.2: Water Resources of India and Odisha

(In billion cubic metres)

Sl. No.	*Description*	*India*	*Odisha**
1.	Annual precipitation	4000	230.76
2.	Average annual water resources	1869	141.40
3.	Utilizable water resources (Surface and ground)	122	108.14
4.	Utilizable resources (% of precipitation)	28%	47%

* includes resources available from outside.

Source: Department of Water Resources, Government of Odisha.

Per-capita Water Availability

The per-capita water availability in the State is reducing progressively owing to increase in population. In 2001, the average per-capita water availability (both surface and ground) in the State was around 3,359 cubic metre (cum) per year, as compared to the national average of 1,820 cum. With the projected future population, the per-capita water availability in the State will reduce to 2,218 cum in 2051. Per-capita water availability less than 1,700 cum is termed water stress condition and while if it falls below 1,000 cum, it is termed as water scarce condition. Though per-capita availability of water resources in our State is relatively favourable in the aggregate, the Rushikulya basin may experience a scarcity condition and basins like Budhabalanga and Bahuda will be close to scarcity condition by 2051. The water requirement of the

State for various purposes in the year 2001 and the projected requirement for the year 2051 is given in Table 4.3.

Table 4.3: Water Requirements for Various Uses in Odisha

(in BCM)

Sl.No.	*Uses*	*Year 2001*			*Year 2051*		
		Surface	*Ground*	*Total*	*Surface*	*Ground*	*Total*
1.	Domestic	0.798	1.198	1.196	1.202	1.803	3.006
2.	Agriculture	18.000	4.688	22.668	40.000	9.408	49.408
3.	Industry	0.606	0.100	0.706	1.750	0.200	1.950
4.	Environment	21.000	8.400	29.400	21.000	8.400	29.400
5.	Others	0.100	0.100	0.200	0.200	0.200	0.400
	Total	**40.504**	**14.486**	**54.990**	**64.152**	**20.010**	**84.463**

Source: Department of Water Resources, Government of Odisha.

Water Storage

In our State a storage capacity of 17.00 BCM has so far been developed through major, medium and minor (flow) projects. Besides the projects under construction will contribute to an additional 1.47 BCM. The details are given in Table 4.4.

Table 4.4: Reservoir Storage Status of Odisha as on 31.03.2009

(in BCM)

Sl.No.	*Category*	*Completed Projects*		*Projects under Construction*	
		No.	*Capacity*	*No.*	*Capacity*
1.	Major	7	14.86	4	1.04
2.	Medium	38	1.30	9	0.43
3.	Minor	2340	0.85	—	—
	Total	**2385**	**17.01**	**13**	**1.47**

Source: Department of Water Resources, Government of Odisha.

Irrigation Scenario

Odisha is primarily an agrarian State. Irrigation holds key to Odisha's economic development and poverty alleviation. The State has a cultivable land of 61.65 lakh ha. It has been assessed that 49.90 lakh ha can be brought under irrigation through major, medium and minor irrigation (flow and lift) irrigation projects (Department of Water Resources, Government of Odisha).

Irrigation development has not made much headway in the State in the pre-independence era. Hardly 183.07 thousand hectares net irrigation potential was created. After introduction of five year plan by Government of India in 1951, attempts were made for rapid harnessing of water resources and much emphasis was laid to accelerate the irrigation potential creation. By the end of March 2009, net irrigation potential of 2,301.35 thousand hectare has been created through major, medium and minor irrigation projects executed by Department of Water Resources. In addition to the above, 533.28 thousand hectare of net irrigation potential was created through other sources like dug well, water harvesting structures, small check dams, etc. Sector-wise created irrigation command up to end of March 2009 is given in Table 4.5.

Table 4.5: Net Irrigation Potential of Odisha as on 31.03.2009

(in thousand hectares)

Sl. No.	*Sector*	*Irrigation Potential*
1.	Major and Medium	1285.93
2.	Minor (Flow)	541.71
3.	Minor (Lift)	473.71
4.	Other Sources	533.28
	Total	**2834.63**

Source: Department of Water Resources, Government of Odisha.

District Profile

Koraput is one of the thirty districts of Odisha situated on the Eastern Ghats regions of South Odisha. It is a tribal dominated district; tribals constitute 49.62 per cent of the total population of the district. It is a landlocked hilly district situated at an altitude of 966 mtrs above mean sea level. The region has a rich geographical diversity abounding stupendous hills, dense forests (although the forest area is fast declining), wild meadows, picturesque waterfalls, terraced valleys and eternal springs. This land of nature's abundance has home to Odisha's vast ethnic tribal population. This district was carved out of the old undivided Koraput district when it was bifurcated into four districts as Koraput, Nabarangpur, Rayagada and Malkangiri in the year 1993.

This district is extending from 18.13° to 19.10° North latitude and 82.5° to 83.23° East longitude covering an area of 8,807 sq.km. It is surrounded by the districts of Bastar (Chhattisgarh) in the west, Nabarangpur district in the north, Rayagada district in the north-east, Srikakulam of Andhra Pradesh in the south-east and Vishakhapatnam district to the south and Malkangiri to the south-west. The district comprises of 2 Sub-divisions, 14 Tehsils and 14 Community Development (CD) Blocks. There are 2,028 revenue villages in the district out of which 1,922 villages are inhabited villages and 106 villages are uninhabited. The district is known for its high concentration of tribal population which constitutes nearly half of its total population. The uniqueness of this district is that 16 tribes are present here which account for 7.4 per cent of the total tribal population of the State.

The total geographical area of the district is 8,807 square kms. The topography consists of high land plateau with a number of hills and hillocks forming parts of Eastern Ghats with the altitude ranging from 300 to 3,000 feet above Mean Sea Level (MSL). The district is an undulating hilly area with high altitude table lands, plateaus and deep river valleys. The hills forms a part of the eastern ghat hill ranges which run in south-west to north-east direction forming part of the heart of the district. The mean elevation is 2,900 feet above mean sea level. The highest peak in Odisha, Deomali with an elevation of 1,672 mtrs is only 35 kms away from the district headquarters.

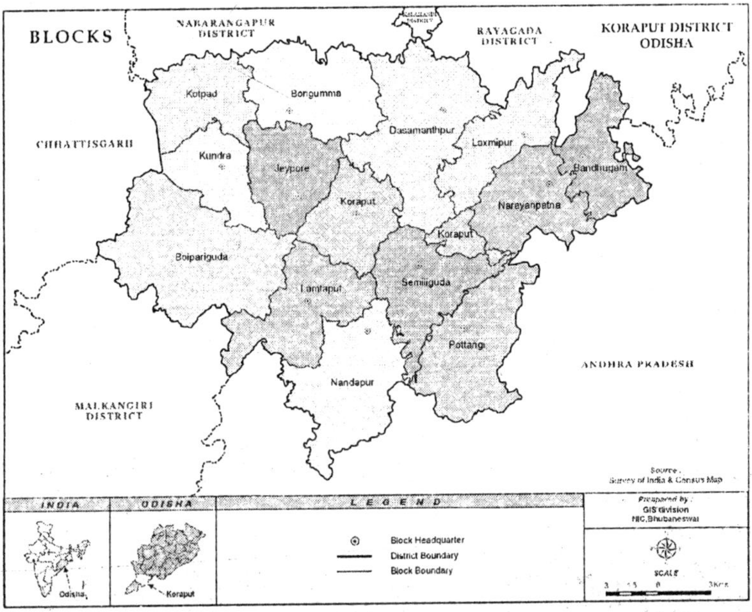

Map 4.2: District Map of Koraput

Soil and Minerals

The soil of this area are mostly occupied with laterite, brown soil and deep sandy loam to clayey loam with low organic matter, saline and slightly acidic in nature. The soils are acidic and poor in fertility. They are highly eroded, rich in iron and aluminium and are usually deficient in Boron and Zinc. In most of the blocks of this district, the soil acidity and iron toxicity are the major problems of the soil.

The forest cover is of deciduous variety covering an area of 1,879.53 square kilometre covering 21.34 per cent of the total area. The various types of forest of this area are Reserved forest 487.86 sq.km., Demarcated protected forest 984.58 sq.km., unclassified forest 0.68 sq.km. and other forest 415.41 sq.km. The mineral wealth of the area includes Bauxite, Black Granite, Graphite, Quartz, Lime Stone, Dolomite, Mica and Clay.

Rivers, Water Falls and Dams

The district has a general slope towards south and west direction. Hence, all the major rivers drain westwards into the basin of Godavari through the tributaries. The rivers like the Indravati, the Kolab, the Machkund, the Guradi and the Patal are the important streams of this district. Besides these streams the hilly terrain has been responsible for the development of a large number of small effluents and *nullahs* with steep gradients which carry the torrential overland flow into these mainstreams. The river beds are filled with boulders, pebbles and gravels which bring disastrous situations during flash floods in rainy season. The Upper Kolab, the Machakund and the Indravati are the major rivers of the district used for irrigation and production of hydro-electricity power.

Climate

The climate of the district is warm and humid with mean maximum and minimum temperature of 30.6 °C and 17.03 °C respectively. April and May are the hottest months and December and January are the coldest months. The temperature in this district ranges from 1 degree Celsius in winter to 44 degrees in summer at some places. The monsoon sets in June. The average annual rainfall of the district is 1,521.8 mm and rainy days are approximately 80 days. June, July, August and September are the usual monsoon months where 79 per cent of the rainfall is recorded in about 60 days. This area is influenced by depressions from Bay of Bengal particularly during the months of September and October.

Storms accompanied by heavy rains frequently occur during monsoons. After rains, floods come in rivers, which cause overflowing of the banks and damage the crops in the valleys. The district also suffers from severe droughts caused by the failure of the rains during some years and other type of natural calamities such as landslides and epidemics. Based on the variation of the topography, soil type, availability of irrigation and cropping patterns, the district is divided into two agro-climatic zones, i.e. Eastern Ghat Highland Zone and low lying South-Eastern Ghat Zone.

Demography

The population of the district is 11.8 lakh as per the 2001 Census and constitutes 3.3 per cent of the total population of the State (Table 4.6). The district has a total number of 2,84,876 households of which 84.3 per cent are rural and 14.7 per cent are urban. The average household size is 4.14 people. The density of population of this district is 134 persons per square kilometre area which is quite low in comparison to the State average which is 236. The decadal growth rate of population is 11.40 per cent during 1991-2001.

The sex ratio is 999 females per every 1,000 males in this district. The sex ratio among the Scheduled Tribe and Scheduled Caste of this district is 1,018 and 1,006 respectively. The overall literacy rate of the district is 35.70 per cent which constitutes 47.2 per cent for male and 24.2 per cent for females which is much lower than the State figures. The rural literacy rate in the district is 27.30 per cent and urban literacy is 74.90 per cent.

Table 4.6: Demographic Indicators of Koraput District *vis-à-vis* Odisha

(Census Report, 2001)

Sl.No.	*Indicators*	*Koraput District*	*Odisha*
(1)	*(2)*	*(3)*	*(4)*
1.	Population	11,80,637	3,68,04,660
	Scheduled Caste (%)	13.04	16.53
	Scheduled Tribe (%)	49.62	22.13
2.	Sex Ratio (females for every 1,000 males)	999	972
3.	Decadal Growth Rate (%) (1991-2001)	11.40	16.25
4.	Literacy rate (%)		
	Total	35.70	63.08
	Males	47.20	75.35
	Females	24.30	50.51
	Rural	27.30	59.84
	Urban	74.90	80.84
5.	Population in age group 0-6 yrs (%)	17.00	14.56
	Male	17.05	14.71
	Female	16.94	14.41

(Contd.)

Table 4.6 (*Contd.*)

(1)	(2)		(3)	(4)
6.	(a)	Work participation rate (%)		
		Total	48.46	38.88
		Male	56.43	52.75
		Female	40.48	24.62
		Rural	51.70	40.33
		Urban	32.45	30.66
	(b)	Main Worker (%)		
		Total	29.95	26.08
		Male	44.76	43.07
		Female	15.13	8.60
	(c)	Marginal Workers (%)		
		Total	18.51	12.80
		Male	11.67	9.68
		Female	25.35	16.02
	(d)	Cultivators (%)	32.71	29.69
		Agricultural Labourers	40.24	35.04
		Household Industry Workers	1.94	4.83
		Other Workers	25.11	30.44
	(e)	Non-Workers (%)		
		Total	51.54	61.12
		Male	43.57	47.25
		Female	59.52	75.38

Source: Statistical Outline of Odisha, 2008.

Scheduled Tribe Population

Koraput district is the abode of several Scheduled Tribe communities. These people love to live amidst picturesque settings comprising rolling mountains, hills, green forests, difficult terrains, plateaus of varying heights, roaring rivers, jumping hill streams, rapid waterfalls, vast stretches of water reservoirs, etc.

The entire district of Koraput is part of the Fifth Schedule area of the State with nearly 50 per cent of tribal component in the population of the district. Almost every tribal community of the State more or less, has recorded its presence in the population of Koraput. However, tribes especially indigenous to Koraput are the Kandha, the Paraja, the Bhottada, the Gadaba, the Bhumia, the Kandadora, the Omanatya, the Perenga, the Kotia, and the Pentia. These communities have sizable population and have their specific areas of concentration in the district.

Shifting Cultivation

Shifting cultivation which needs a special mention here, is a distinct type of agriculture, practised mostly by the tribals of undivided Koraput district. It is a system which consists of cutting of trees on tops and slopes of hills, burning the fallow trees and bushes and lastly dibbling or broadcasting seeds in the ash covered soil. The land so prepared is cultivated for two to three years till its fertility is exhausted. Then the land is abandoned and a new patch of forest land is brought under cultivation. The cultivation is thus shifted from one patch to another after every few years of cultivation.

In the local language shifting cultivation is popularly known as 'Podu' cultivation. Some of the characteristics of Podu cultivation are the rotation of the fields, use of fire as cleaning agent, use of human labour as chief input, use of simple tools like dibble stick or hoe, practice of mixed cropping in the land, etc. Although production of food crops is the main type of agricultural practice among the tribals under shifting cultivation, some cash and commercial crops are also raised. As the shifting cultivation is entirely dependent on the rainwater, the productivity varies depending on the quantity and timing of the rainfall. The tribal people depend on other collection of forest produce, hunting and gathering of food for the rest of the year. In some cases they work as casual labourers to earn their living.

Land Utilization Pattern

Out of the 8.8 lakh hectares of land in the district only 34.18 per cent is the net sown area. The categorization of land is of three types, i.e. high, medium, low. Out of the total agricultural land of 3,02,000 hectares, 1,66,000 ha is of high, 78,000 ha is medium and 58,000 ha is of low category. Paddy is cultivated in 7,000 ha of high land, 50,000 ha in medium and 58,000 ha of low category land.

The distribution of landholding is very peculiar in this district as tribals dominate the agriculture sector. The small and marginal farmers having land below two hectares are 69 per cent of the total number of farmers having only 34 per cent of the total land ownership. On the other hand, the medium and large farmers which constitute 31 per cent of the total farmers have as much as 66 per cent of the total land under their possession. There are about 40 per cent of the landless agricultural labourers out of the total working population of the district.

Cropping Pattern

A majority of the farmers of the district cultivate on the dongar land and follow the basic cropping pattern, i.e. rainfed upland paddy, *ragi*, millets and niger sown in a sequential manner on the foothills and dongar lands. The slope gradient of the dongar lands vary from 3 per cent to 15 per cent. Paddy is the major crop of the region occupying about 50 per cent of the net sown area and it is the staple diet of the local people. It is believed that rice has its origin from undivided Koraput district. Upland paddy and ragi are cultivated on around one-third of the sloping land. In the hilly areas of the district traditional cultivation along the streambed called *jhola* cultivation is used for growing paddy. The *jhola* system are the sophisticated water management systems where terracing, levelling and channelling of perennial stream provide sufficient water and nutrition for paddy cultivation, mostly without use of fertilizers. Medium and uplands are used for the upland paddy and various other crops, whereas hill slopes with high gradient are used for shifting cultivation. The land use pattern is dynamic, i.e. new land is created along the stream beds and rotational agriculture is followed on hill slopes.

The technology used by the farmers of the district is old and obsolete for the cultivation and production. The traditional plough and bullock method of cultivation is still in use in the interior parts of the district. The use of intensive methods of cultivation is not practiced due to the use of traditional methods of cultivation. Several factors which are responsible for this is that of uneconomic holding, lack of financial capacity and ignorance of the farmers. As a result of which the per hectare yield is much lower in comparison to the state and national average. The use of chemical fertilizers, pesticides and insecticides are very much limited to a few well irrigated blocks of Kotpad, Jeypore, Kundra and Borigumma. For most of the farmers of the rainfed areas agriculture is subsistence.

Irrigation

Out of the total agricultural land of the district only 42.56 per cent of the area is irrigated by all sources of irrigation. This has been possible due to some of the major and minor irrigation projects including water harvesting structures. Out of the total area irrigated 43 per cent are by major irrigation projects, 7 per cent by medium irrigation projects, 12 per cent by minor irrigation projects and 38 per cent by other sources which includes the water sources created out of block, ITDA, NREGA, BKY and BRGF funds (Minor Irrigation Department, Government of Odisha). In the district Jeypore block has the highest irrigation facility (94.24%) and Boipariguda block is the least irrigated area (9.78%) of the district.

After the implementation of the watershed development programmes during 1998-99 in various parts of the district there has been a perceptible change in crop diversification from paddy to non-paddy crops. Cash crops like Cashew, Coffee, Ginger and vegetables are replacing cereal crops like paddy and wheat. In Semiliguda and Pottangi blocks due to the availability of water from the watershed projects a lot of vegetables like cauliflower, cabbage, tamato, radish, chillies, beans, cucumber, etc. are produced in plenty and the quantity of yield per hectare has also increased to a marked extent.

Agriculture Finance

Indebtedness is a major problem of the farmers particularly among the tribal cultivators of the district. Living in a subsistence economy, the tribals go for loan against the mortgage of land. Loans are obtained from moneylenders and traders at very high rate of interest due to the non-availability of the institutional finances. On the ground that inability to pay the loan along with the interest, the farmers are compelled to part away with their land.

The marketing of agricultural products is a big problem for the farmers in our country as the farmers have to sell their products at a very cheap price due to lack of storage facilities and urgent need of money. The farmers of this district are also no exception to it. The price of perishable commodities fluctuates depending on the demand and supply factors without the storage facilities. The illiterate and ignorant farmers have to suffer during bumper crops at the hands of the middleman as they have to sell their commodities at prices which is much below the official support price fixed by the government due to the urgent need for money. The illiterate farmers are also exploited at the hands of unscrupulous traders in respect of weight and measures. Koraput district is famous for producing good quality turmeric and ginger but due to lack of marketing support the farmers have to sell their products at very low prices which discourage them to produce the same crop again in future. There is very few availability of cold storage facility in this district for the farmers which cause hardship among the farmers for the storage of perishable commodities.

Horticulture and Cash Crops

Koraput district has been identified as one of the most ideal location for the horticulture. The agro-climatic condition of the district is quite conducive for the production of many fruits and vegetables all through the year. Many fruits like jackfruit, mango, guava, sapota, litchi, pomegranate, custard apple, papaya, cashew nut, aonla, banana, pineapple, lemon, etc. are produced in various parts of the district.

Koraput district has the distinction of producing good quality coffee. As per estimates given by the coffee board, 957 hectares of land is under coffee cultivation producing 256 metric tonne of coffee. The average yield of coffee is estimated at 950 kg per hectare. As the plantation of coffee requires a good amount of investment and a longer gestation period, the small and marginal farmers are not able to take advantage of this crop due to non-availability of financial support to them.

Animal Husbandry

Animal Husbandry is the mainstay of rainfed farmers particularly in drought prone, arid and semi-arid areas. The farmers of this area need support of animal husbandry for a sustainable income generation throughout the year. A majority of the rural small, marginal and landless labourers are benefitted from the additional income from the livestock like dairy farming, sheep, goat rearing and poultry farming.

Development of Micro-Watersheds

Background: Watershed is a geo-hydrological unit wherein the water drains into a common point. Watershed management aims at harmonious development and management of soil and water resources within the natural boundary of a watershed so as to develop and produce on a sustainable basis, crops, vegetation, livestock, etc. for equitable sharing of benefits among the communities living within the watershed. It focuses towards harnessing and conserving land balance. Various soil and water conservation interventions are taken up so as to improve and develop the natural, animal and human resources falling within the watershed. The Koraput district is part of the Koraput-Bolangir-Kalahandi (KBK) area where the Long Term Action Plan (LTAP) of the Central Government is being implemented. This region of Odisha is considered as one of the most backward areas of the country. About 50 per cent of the population of the area belong to ST population. The Central Government as well as the State government is implementing various programmes for the development of these underprivileged people.

Status of Watershed Programme in KBK Districts: Watershed Development Programmes are currently being implemented in the state under various centrally sponsored schemes like Drought Prone Area Programme (DPAP), Integrated Wasteland Development Programme (IWDP), National Wasteland Development Programme for Rainfed Areas (NWDPRA), River Valley Projects (RVP) Rashtriya Krishi Vikas Yojana (RKVY), etc. The Watershed Development Programme is also implemented under special plan (RLTAP) for KBK districts. Besides, one externally aided project, i.e. Western Odisha Rural Livelihoods Project (WORLP) funded by DFID, is also being implemented in four districts namely Bolangir, Nuapada, Kalahandi and Bargarh.

Recently, Odisha Livelihoods Programme called JEEBIKA has been started in six districts of the State namely, Koraput, Malkangiri, Nabarangpur and Rayagada, Kandhamal and Mayurbhanj in order to provide additional livelihoods not only to the landless households but also the poorest and vulnerable sections by developing alternative and diversified livelihood opportunities.

Status of Watershed Development Programmes in KBK Districts

(i) *National Watershed Development Programme for Rainfed Area (NWDPRA):* The NWDPRA is being implemented as a component of the CSP Macro Management of Agriculture. The broad objective of the scheme is natural resource management for enhancement of agricultural productivity and production of biomass on a sustainable basis and restoration of ecological balance in rainfed areas through watershed approach. The cost is shared as 90 per cent by the Central Government and 10 per cent by the State Government. Out of the Central share, 80 per cent is provided as grant and 20 per cent as loan to the State. During Eleventh Plan, 66 micro-watersheds have been taken up in KBK districts under NWDPRA for treatment of 32,377 hectares of area. During the year 2008-09, a sum of ₹ 276.34 lakh has been utilized by treating an area of 2,298 ha. It is proposed to implement the ongoing 66 watersheds in KBK districts during the year 2009-10 with an estimated cost of ₹ 396.33 lakh for treatment of 3,630 ha.

(ii) *River Valley Project (RVP):* The RVP is being implemented as a component of Macro-Management of Agriculture. The Government of India provides 90 per cent of the funds as the Central share and the balance 10 per cent as the State share. The RVP scheme aims at treating degraded catchment area of the multipurpose interstate reservoirs with appropriate soil and water conservation measures to check silt inflow into reservoirs and to enhance the productivity of degraded land. The scheme is in operation in four catchments of the state, i.e. Hirakud, Rengali-Mandira, Upper Kolab and Upper Indravati. During 2008-09, a sum of ₹ 287.36 lakh has been utilized for treatment of 4,456 ha area in 9 watersheds in Upper Kolab and Indravati catchments. During 2009-10, it is proposed to implement the ongoing 9 watersheds in KBK districts with an outlay of 1,895 ha area.

(iii) *Drought Prone Area Programme (DPAP):* The DPAP is in operation in 8 districts of Odisha covering 47 identified blocks. The districts covered are Bolangir, Boudh, Dhenkanal and Kandhmal. Under the scheme 1,319 Micro-Watershed projects are under implementation and 192 projects have been completed in Bolangir, Subarnapur and Kalahandi districts. Those 192 projects were sanctioned prior to 01.04.2000 with the funding pattern of 50:50 basis at the cost norm of ₹ 4,000 (₹ 5,000 for KBK districts) per ha. The remaining project have been sanctioned after 01.04.2000 with the funding pattern of 75:25 basis at the new cost norm of ₹ 6,000 per ha on an uniform basis. In the four KBK districts, 778 watersheds have been taken up with a target area of 3,88,809 ha. By the end of 2008-09, a sum of ₹ 10,390.47 lakh has been utilized with treatment of 1,65,085 ha of area.

(iv) *Integrated Watershed Development Programme (IWDP):* The Integrated Wasteland Development Programme (IWDP) scheme is being implemented in 23 districts except Puri, Jagatsingpur, Bhadrak, Kendrapada, Boudh, Kandhamal and Nuapada. Under the scheme 1,046 Micro-Watershed Projects are under implementation out of which 246 projects sanctioned prior to 01.04.2000 with 100 per cent grant. After 01.04.2000, the funding pattern between the Government of India and State Government is in ratio of 11:1 at the new cost norm of ₹ 6,000 per ha (₹ 5,500 as Central share and ₹ 500 as State share). In the KBK districts, 377 watersheds have been taken up with the targeted area of 2,09,721 ha. By end of 2008-09, a sum of ₹ 6,410 lakh has been utilized with treatment of 1,20,180 ha area.

(v) *Western Odisha Rural Livelihoods Project (WORLP):* The Western Odisha Rural Livelihoods Project (WORLP) was launched during 2000-01 with assistance from DFID, to cover 290 Micro-watersheds, 29 blocks and 545 villages in the 4 project districts of the State namely, i.e. Bolangir, Nuapada, Kalahandi and Bargarh districts over a period of 10 years. The project aim at promoting sustainable rural livelihoods for the poorest in the project area through watershed plus activities and would support land and water management, livelihoods initiatives for the poorest, capacity building and encourage an enabling environment to address Government policy. The project is currently under operation in 14 blocks of Bolangir, 5 blocks of Nuapada, 6 blocks of Kalahandi and 4 blocks of Bargarh districts. The project follows the common guidelines of the Ministry of Rural Development for implementation of the watershed activities. The watershed plus component under the WORLP has an additional cost of ₹ 3,500 per ha. for promoting livelihoods among the poorest in the project area. Under the scheme, 250 watersheds have been taken up in the KBK districts with targeted area of 1.25 lakh for treatment. All the projects are currently ongoing and ₹ 9,395.88 lakh has been utilized by the end of 2008-09 with treatment of 76,266 ha. area.

(vi) *Odisha Rural Livelihoods Programme (ORLP):* The Odisha Rural Livelihoods Programme (ORLP) is an initiative for providing an additional livelihood component to 460 ongoing watershed projects under IWDP and DPAP in the state covering six districts such as Koraput, Nabrangpur, Rayagada, Malkangiri, Kandhamal and Mayurbhanj. This programme, called the JEEBIKA, intends to address and enhance the livelihood needs of landless and marginal households that are generally left out under normal watershed activities. The additional livelihoods component or the watershed plus would be integrated into the existing watershed projects in consecutive three years starting from 2007-08 to 2009-10 with a total provision of ₹ 9,046.96 lakh so that the benefits flow not only to the landed households but also to the poorest and vulnerable sections, by developing alternative and diversified livelihoods opportunities.

Status of Watershed Development Programmes in Koraput District

The Koraput district comprises four Catchments namely (1) Indravati, (2) Machakund, (3) Kolab, and (4) Nagavali. The details of number of sub-catchments, Watersheds, Sub-watershed, Mini Watershed and approximate area of the above four catchments is given in Table 4.7. The watershed map of Koraput district is shown in Map 4.3.

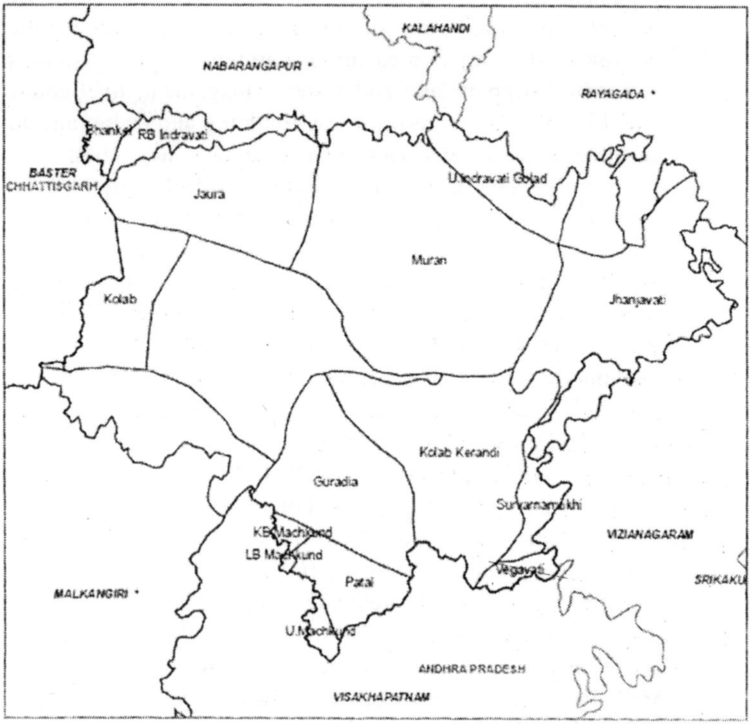

Map 4.3: Watershed Map of Koraput District

Table 4.7: River Catchments of Koraput District

Name of the Catchment	*No. of Catchments*	*No. of Watershed*	*No. of Sub-Watershed*	*No. of Mini Watershed*	*Area in Ha*	*No. of Micro-Watersheds*
Indravati	3	8	73	132	1,77,295	355
Machkund	1	2	16	32	46,920	94
Kolab	4	12	109	279	3,29,907	660
Nagavali	2	4	43	88	1,13,610	227
Total	**10**	**26**	**241**	**521**	**6,67,732**	**1,336**

Source: DRDA, Koraput.

The Watershed Development Programme has been taken up in the district since Eighth Plan period with the introduction of NWDPRA.

Subsequently, watersheds have been taken up under IWDP, RVP, EAS and ACA. Besides, watershed development programme have also been taken up by the Non-Governmental Organizations of the district with financial assistance from various funding agencies like CAPART, NABARD and also in collaboration with the external agencies. Besides all these, five watersheds in the district has also been taken up with the financial assistance of Denmark Government through a project named IDCWDP.

Details of completed and ongoing Watershed Projects in Koraput District up to April, 2015 is shown in Table 4.8.

Profile of the Study Blocks

Laxmipur Block

Laxmipur block has a geographical area of 311.18 sq.km. It has 13 numbers of gram panchayats and 103 revenue villages. This block has 100 numbers of hamlets. The population of the block is 55,268 as per the 2001 Census. The density of population is 178 per square kilometre in the block. The literacy rate is only 27.71 per cent of the total population. In the whole block there are 13,600 households (2001 Census) and the number of BPL families (1997) is 12,688, which is about 88 per cent of the total households. The total number of retail shop under public distribution system is 66.

The net sown area of the block is 8,327 hectares (2006-07). The forest area is 1,447 hectares. The irrigated area of the block is 5,181 hectares (Rabi 2,584 and Kharif 2,597) and culturable wasteland is 1,100 hectares. The rainfall in the block was 1,958.7 mm in 2006 and the water table was 3.70 metres minimum and 21.20 maximum. The yield rate of paddy was 28.75 qntls/ha in 2006-07. As per the official statistics the entire block is covered under drinking water project. The number of working tubewells is 516, sanitary wells 87 and number of piped water projects in the block is 8. The total number of Watershed Projects completed/ongoing in the block is 26 in numbers. These projects have been undertaken in the block under various schemes which includes 10 numbers of watershed projects by CYSD under the OTELP programme.

Borigumma Block

The total geographical area of the block is 605.58 sq.km. The numbers of Gram Panchayats is 30 and the number of revenue villages 148 and

Table 4.8: Watershed Programmes Undertaken in Koraput District (completed/ongoing) up to April 2015

Sl.No.	*Scheme*	*No. of Watersheds*	*Outlay (₹ lakh)*	*Amount Allotted (₹)*	*Expenditure Made (₹ lakh)*	*Area Treated/ Treatable (hectares)*	*Period*	*Project Status*
1.	EAS	72	1,440.00	1,140.02	1,134.50	2,6932.00	1998-99 to 2002-03	Completed
2.	IDCWDP	05	338.67	338.67	NA	16430.00	1993-94 to 2002-03	Completed
3.	ACA	84	2,484.00	2,280.40	2,216.78	3,6438.00	2002-03 to 2006-07	Completed
4.	IWDP I-III	03	278.46	268.52	266.34	3,873.00	1993-94 to 2002-03	Completed
5.	IWDP-IV	24	481.80	480.72	480..72	1,1624.00	1998-99 to 2002-03	Completed
6.	IWDP-V	10	300.00	225.00	222.30	3535.00	2006-07 to 2010-11	Completed
7.	IWDP-VI	10	300.00	45.00	44.70	670.00	2006-07 to 2010-11	Completed
8.	IWDP-VII	10	300.00	45.00	44.70	705.00	2003-04 to 2008-09	Completed
9.	SCA	35	1,662.50	947.41	679.15	4,630.00	2008-09 to 2012-13	Completed
10.	OTELP-I	30	2,222.07	2,138.46	1,892.17	15,208.68	2005-06 to 2011-12	Completed
11.	OTELP-II	40	3,009.96	536.90	356.90	2,0601.18	2008-09 to 2014-15	Ongoing
12.	IWMP I to V	60	3,600.00	669.60	174.11	3,0000.00	2009-10 to 2015-16	Ongoing
13.	IWMP VI-VII	19	1,440.00	726.00	708.51	5904.24	2010-11 to 2016-17	Ongoing
14.	IWMP VIII-IX	14	1,392.00	515.76	504.04	4201.99	2011-12 to 2017-18	Ongoing
15.	IWMP X-XI	11	1,333.95	541.54	413.27	2755.14	2012-13 to 2018-19	Ongoing
16.	IWMP XII-XIII	14	1,725.00	115.58	90.86	605.72	2013-14 to 2019-20	Ongoing
	Total	**441**	**22,308.41**	**11,014.58**	**8,748.33**	**1,84,113.95**		

Source: Compiled from various watershed implementing agencies, 2015.

the number of hamlets is 288. The total population of the block is 1,26,728 (2001 Census). The density of population in the block is 209 and the literacy rate is 32.76 per cent. The total number of households is 31,026 (2001) and number of BPL families in the block is 31,453 which is 87 per cent of the total population of the block (BPL Census, 1997). The rainfall in this block is 1088.3 mm in 2006. The water table of this block is minimum 5.00 metres and maximum 24.00 metres in the year 2005-06.

The culturable wasteland of this block was 3,873 ha in 2006-07 and the forest area in 2006-07 was 3,823 ha. The net sown area of this block was 2757 ha in 2006-07. The irrigated area of the block as on 2007-08 was 15,435 ha (*Rabi* 5,345 ha and *Kharif* 10,090 ha). Paddy which is the main crop of the area has an average yield of 26.61 qntl/ha in this block. The total number of watershed Projects completed/ongoing in the block is 20 in numbers. These projects have been undertaken in the block under various schemes of the State and Central Government. There are 1,263 numbers of working tubewell covering 313 villages of the block. There are 73 sanitary wells and 19 piped water projects in the block.

Boipariguda Block

The total geographical area of the block is 764.84 sq.km. The number of Gram Panchayats is 16, number of revenue villages is 279 and the number of hamlets is 324. The total population of the block is 91,621 (2001 Census). The density of population in the block is 120 and the literacy rate is 21.07 per cent. The total number of households is 22,832 (Census, 2001) and number of BPL families in the block is 19,396 which is 82 per cent of the total population of the block (1997). The rainfall in this block is 2,064.0 mm in 2006. The water table of this block was minimum 3.10 metres and maximum 15.15 metres in the year 2005-06.

The culturable wasteland of this block was 1,321 ha in 2006-07 and the forest area was 23,646 ha in 2006-07. The net sown area of this block was 22,584 ha in 2006-07. The irrigated area of the block as on 2007-08 was 2946 ha (*Rabi* 936 ha and *Kharif* 2,010 ha). Paddy which is the main crop of the area has an average yield of 20.76 qntl/ha in this block. The total number of Watershed Projects completed/ongoing in the block is 31 in numbers. These projects have been undertaken in the block under various schemes of the State and Central Government. There are 999 numbers of working tubewells covering 487 villages of the block. There are 99 sanitary wells and 9 piped water projects in the block.

Semiliguda Block

Semiliguda block has a geographical area of 313.56 sq.km. It has 16 numbers of gram panchayats and 85 revenue villages. This block has 172 numbers of hamlets. The population of the block is 55,537 as per the 2001 census. The density of population is 177 per square kilometre in the block. The literacy rate is only 24.33 per cent of the total population. In the entire block, there are 14,026 households (2001 Census) and the number of BPL families (1997) is 12,784, which is about 86 per cent of the total households. The total number of retail shops under public distribution system is 80.

The net sown area of the block is 11,261 hectares (2006-07). The forest area is 627 hectares. The total irrigated area of the block is 7,438 hectares (*Rabi* 35,984 and *Kharif* 3,840) and culturable wasteland is 1,435 hectares. The rainfall in the block was 2,577 mm in 2006 and the water table was 6.00 metres minimum and 17.50 maximum. The yield rate of paddy was 28.75 qntls/ha in 2006-07. As per the official statistics the entire block is covered under drinking water project. The number of working tubewells is 394, sanitary wells 232 and number of piped water projects in the block is 7. The total number of Watershed Projects completed/ongoing in the block is 38 in numbers. These projects have been undertaken in the block under various schemes which includes 10 numbers of watershed projects by TSRD (NGO) under the OTELP programme.

Pottangi Block

This block has a geographical area of 257.72 sq.km. It has 14 numbers of gram panchayats and 100 revenue villages. This block has 410 numbers of hamlets. The population of the block is 60,300 as per the 2001 Census. The density of population is 234 per square kilometre in the block. The literacy rate is only 21.11 per cent of the total population. In the whole block there are 13,739 households (2001 Census) and the number of BPL families (1997) is 13,588, which is about 85 per cent of the total households. The total number of retail shops under public distribution system is 38.

The net sown area of the block is 8,701 hectares (2006-07). The forest area is 5,478 hectares. The irrigated area of the block is 5,275 hectares (*Rabi* 2,217 ha and *Kharif* 3,058 ha) and culturable wasteland is 1,160 hectares. The rainfall in the block was 2,584.4 mm in 2006 and the water table was 6.70 metres minimum and 17.85 metres maximum.

The yield rate of paddy was 28.36 qntls/ha in 2006-07. As per the official statistics, the entire block is covered under drinking water project. The number of working tubewells is 446, sanitary wells 321 and number of piped water projects in the block is 7. The total number of Watershed Projects completed/ongoing in the block is 38 in numbers. These projects have been undertaken in the block under various schemes of the State and Central Government which includes 10 numbers of watershed projects by LAVS (NGO) under the OTELP programme.

The detail of the watershed projects undertaken in the five sample blocks of Koraput district is given in Table 4.9.

Table 4.9: Scheme-wise WDPs Taken up in Five Sample Blocks of Koraput District

Sl.No.	*Scheme*	*Semiliguda*	*Pottangi*	*Borigumma*	*Boipariguda*	*Laxmipur*	*Status*
1.	EAS	04	05	06	06	05	Completed
2.	ACA	06	06	06	06	06	Completed
3.	IWDP	07	Nil	Nil	Nil	01	Completed
4.	SCA	Nil	05	05	05	05	Completed
5.	IWMP	12	12	Nil	12	Nil	Ongoing
6.	IDCWDP	Nil	Nil	03	02	Nil	Completed
7.	OTELP	10	10	Nil	Nil	10	Ongoing
	Total	**39**	**38**	**20**	**31**	**27**	

Source: Compiled from data collected from various implementing Agencies, 2010.

5

WATERSHED DEVELOPMENT PROGRAMME
A Sample Study

The Background

There have been a number of studies conducted on the impact and evaluation of watershed development programmes in various parts of the country. In this study, the area selected for the study is one of the most backward districts in India which has come under the RLTAP programme of the Central Government. More than 80 per cent of the population of the district, as per the official statistics belongs to below poverty line (BPL) category. At the same time, almost half of the population of the district belong to the Scheduled Tribe and it comes under the fifth schedule area of the State. The literacy rate in the rural areas of the district is abysmally low as compared to the State and the district average. Keeping all these in mind, the Central and State Government are spending huge amount of money through various plans and schemes to enhance the standard of living of these people. The watershed development programme which has been accepted as one of the flagship programmes of the Government for the improvement of livelihood of rainfed area people and increase the productivity in agriculture needs to be reviewed on the basis of its impact on the people of the tribal dominated district of Koraput.

Selection of the Sample

In order to take stock of the situation, the present study was undertaken in the district by the scholar, the year of study being 2008-09. Out of various watershed projects implemented in the district only some of the completed projects have been taken up for an in-depth study. Out of the 14 blocks in the district, five blocks (about 35%) have been taken as the sample size keeping in view the composite development index of these blocks in the district. Some of the most irrigated and least irrigated blocks with different agro-climatic zones of the district have been taken purposively for a comparative evaluation purpose. Four watersheds from each of the above sample blocks have been selected on the random sampling basis which was taken up during the period 1998-99 to 2002-03. The current study is also to make a comparative analysis of the performance of the watershed projects after the project period is over with that of the pre-watershed period. The biophysical aspects and the socio-economic benefits of the projects are assessed through a total sample size of 300 households. For this purpose for the sample, 15 numbers of households from each chosen watersheds are selected randomly and a structured questionnaire prepared exclusively for the purpose was administered. The scholar visited each of the watersheds which comprise one or more than one village and collected information from the households and also conducted focus group discussions with the villagers and discussed with the elected representatives of the village, the watershed committee members and the officers of the line departments of government. As all the watershed projects completed so far have been implemented by the Government agencies, the Programme Implementing Agencies (PIAs) of all the 20 watershed projects selected in the sample belongs to various departments of the Government.

Scheme-wise Watershed Projects and Studies Conducted

The watershed projects implemented so far/ongoing in this district are given in Table 5.1. As it is seen in Table 5.1, the total number of watershed projects already implemented/are being implemented in the district are 383 in number. Out of this 190 number of projects have been completed so far and the rest are at various stages of implementation. The watershed projects are under various schemes like Employment Assurance Scheme (EAS), Additional Central Assistance (ACA), Integrated Wasteland Development Programme (IWDP), Special Central Assistance (SCA) under the RLTAP, Integrated Watershed Management Programme (IWMP) known as JEEBIKA, Odisha Tribal Empowerment and Livelihood Programme (OTELP). All the above schemes except the OTELP are being implemented through the various Government departments. The OTELP watershed projects are implemented through the Non-Governmental Organizations (NGOs). The details of allotment, expenditure, area treated, mandays of labour generated of the twenty sample watershed projects is given in Table 5.2. Out of the twenty

Table 5.1: Status of Watershed Development Projects in Koraput District up to March 2011

Sl.No.	Scheme	No. of Watersheds	Outlay (₹ lakh)	Amount Allotted (₹)	Expenditure Made (₹ lakh)	Area Treated/ Treatable (hectares)	Period	Project Status
1.	EAS	72	1,440.00	1,140.02	1,134.50	26,932	1998-99 to 2002-03	Completed
2.	IDCWDP	05	338.67	338.67	NA	16,430	1993-94 to 2002-03	Completed
3.	ACA	84	2,484.00	2,280.40	2,216.78	36,438	2002-03 to 2006-07	Completed
4.	IWDP I -III	03	278.46	268.52	266.34	3,873	1993-94 to 2002-03	Completed
5.	IWDP-IV	24	481.80	480.72	480.72	11,624	1998-99 to 2002-03	Completed
6.	IWDP-V	10	300.00	225.00	222.30	3,535	2006-07 to 2010-11	Ongoing
7.	IWDP-VI	10	300.00	45.00	44.70	670	2006-07 to 2010-11	Ongoing
8.	IWDP-VII	10	300.00	45.00	44.70	705	2003-04 to 2008-09	Completed
9.	SCA	35	1,662.50	947.41	679.15	4,630	2008-09 to 2012-13	Ongoing
10.	IWMP I to V	60	3,600.00	669.60	174.11	30,000	2009-10 to 2015-16	Ongoing
11.	OTELP-I	30	2,222.07	2,138.46	1,892.17	15,208.68	2005-06 to-2011-12	Ongoing
12.	OTELP-II	40	3,009.96	536.90	356.90	20,601.18	2008-09 to 2014-15	Ongoing
	Total	**383**	**16,417.46**	**9115.70**	**7512.37**	**1,70,646.86**		

Source: Compiled from various watershed implementing agencies, 2010.

Table 5.2: Basic Information about the Sample Watershed Projects Taken under Study

Sl.No.	*Name of the W/S*	*Block*	*Scheme*	*Amount Alloted (₹ lakh)*	*Expenditure Made (₹ lakh)*	*Area Treated (hectares)*	*Labour Mandays Generated (lakh)*
1.	Panasput	Semiliguda	ACA	26.74	26.74	445.67	0.47750
2.	Kankadambo	Semiliguda	ACA	26.74	26.74	445.67	0.47750
3.	Ranikana	Semiliguda	ACA	26.74	26.74	445.67	0.47750
4.	Pomi	Semiliguda	ACA	26.74	26.74	445.67	0.47750
5.	Badaliguda	Pottangi	ACA	27.54	27.54	459.08	0.49188
6.	Badapadu	Pottangi	ACA	27.54	27.54	459.08	0.49188
7.	Girliguda	Pottangi	ACA	27.54	27.54	459.08	0.49188
8.	Malkarbandh*	Pottangi	EAS	17.25	17.25	431.25	0.30804
9.	Jujhari	Borigumma	ACA	26.74	26.74	445.67	0.47750
10.	Khandiguda	Borigumma	ACA	26.74	26.74	445.67	0.47750
11.	Lodijodi	Borigumma	ACA	26.74	26.74	445.67	0.47750
12.	Jodabandh	Borigumma	ACA	26.74	26.74	445.67	0.47750
13.	Nandanmala	Boipariguda	ACA	26.74	26.74	445.67	0.47750
14.	Bodaguda	Boipariguda	ACA	26.74	26.74	445.67	0.47750
15.	Atalguda	Boipariguda	ACA	26.74	26.74	445.67	0.47750
16.	Majhiguda	Boipariguda	ACA	26.74	26.74	445.67	0.47750
17.	Marbaiguda	Laxmipur	ACA	26.74	26.74	445.67	0.47750
18.	Maligaon	Laxmipur	ACA	26.74	26.74	445.67	0.47750
19.	Bandikar	Laxmipur	ACA	26.74	26.74	445.67	0.47750
20.	Timajhola*	Laxmipur	EAS	19.10	19.10	477.50	0.34107
	Total			**520.08**	**520.85**	**8,971.00**	**9.28723**

* The treatable area is smaller than others.

Source: District Rural Development Agency, Koraput, 2010.

watershed projects of five blocks of the district, 18 belong to the Additional Central Assistance (ACA) and the rest two projects belong to Employment Assurance Scheme (EAS). The entire allotted amount for the above projects have been fully utilized by the respective watershed committees.

In Table 5.2 the details of amount allotted, expenditure made and mandays of labour generated of each sample watershed project is given. A structured questionnaire was prepared by the scholar keeping in view the objectives of the study. As the rural areas of the district are inhabitated predominantly by the tribal people and the literacy rate of these people is very low, the researcher has to face a lot of difficulty in explaining the objectives of the study and eliciting answers for questions on the watershed projects.

In Map 5.1, the sample watersheds selected as sample for the study under EAS and ACA scheme have been shown. In Map 5.2, all the watershed projects taken up in the district have been shown.

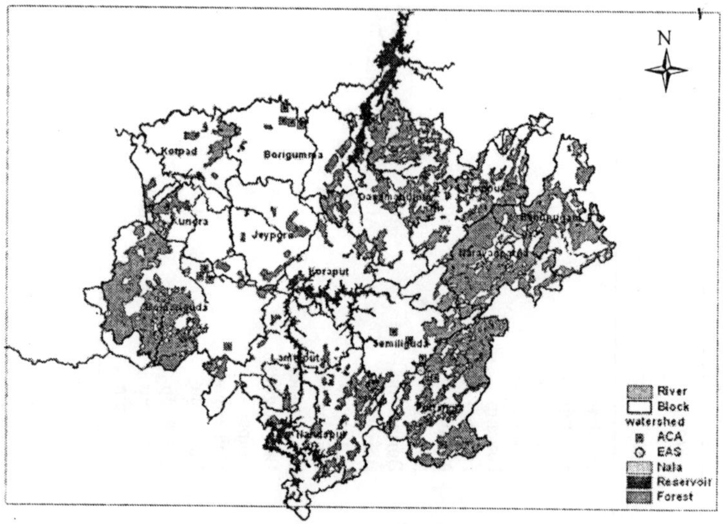

Map 5.1: Sample Watersheds taken for the Study

As mentioned earlier, a structured questionnaire was prepared to elicit answers from the head of the household of the watershed area under study. The tribal communities like the Kondh, the Paraja and the Gadaba are the main tribes of the study area. In order to establish a friendly atmosphere contact and translation of the local dialect for better understanding, the help of some local knowledgeable person was taken.

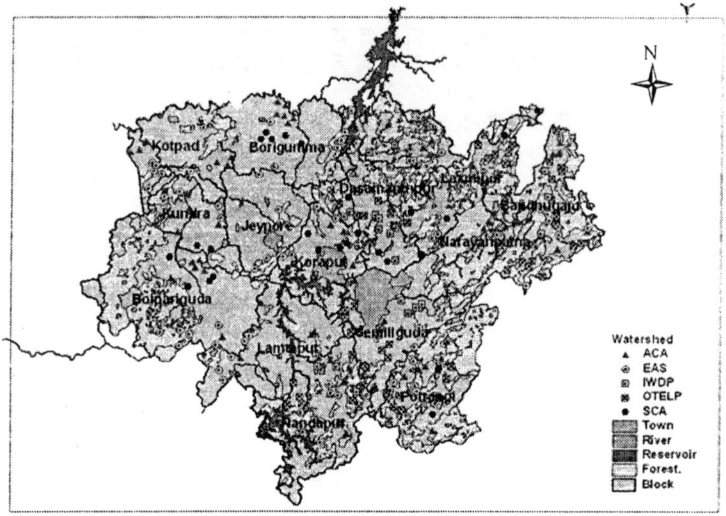

Map 5.2: All Watershed Projects in Koraput District

A common notion among the most of the tribal people is that if someone outsider comes to their village then, he or she must be a Government Official and he/she can provide some kind of help or assistance to them. Keeping this in mind, the scholar tried to explain the purpose of visit and convinced them that the information collected from them would be purely used for academic purpose and in the long-run, when these information collected from them would be published, the authorities would know better their problems and difficulties and then take steps for their solution. In the household survey conducted during 2008-09, it was kept in mind that the sample watershed projects would represent various categories of households like the Scheduled Tribe, Scheduled Caste, landless labourers, user groups, non-user groups, farmers and upstream and downstream users to have a better understanding of the problem. Actually such categories of households were surveyed. A sample questionnaire is annexed in Annexure No. 2.

In Table 5.3, the details of allotment and expenditure on various components of the sample watersheds are given. The total allotment on different components for all the 20 selected sample WDPs was ₹ 520.09 lakh and the total amount was spent on the respective components. The various components on which the allotted amount was spent are Entry Point Activities (EPA), training, community organization, administration and expenditure on various labour intensive works.

Table 5.3: Component-wise Allotment and Expenditure on Sample Watersheds of Koraput District (₹ *in lakh*)

Sl.No.	Name of the W/S	Administrative Expenses		Community Organization		Training		Entry Point Activities (EPA)		Works		Total	
		Allot.	Exp.	Allot.	Exp.	Allot.	Exp.	Allot.	Exp.	Allot.	Exp.	Allot.	Exp.
1.	Panasput	2.40	2.40	1.50	1.50	0.60	0.60	0.00	0.00	22.24	22.24	26.74	26.74
2.	Kankadambo	2.40	2.40	1.50	1.50	0.60	0.60	0.00	0.00	22.24	22.24	26.74	26.74
3.	Ranikana	2.40	2.40	1.50	1.50	0.60	0.60	0.00	0.00	22.24	22.24	26.74	26.74
4.	Pomi	2.40	2.40	1.50	1.50	0.60	0.60	0.00	0.00	22.24	22.24	26.74	26.74
5.	Badaliguda	2.40	2.40	1.50	1.50	0.60	0.60	0.00	0.00	23.05	23.05	27.55	27.55
6.	Badapadu	2.40	2.40	1.50	1.50	0.60	0.60	0.00	0.00	23.05	23.05	27.55	27.55
7.	Girliguda	2.40	2.40	1.50	1.50	0.60	0.60	0.00	0.00	23.05	23.05	27.55	27.55
8.	Malkarbandh	1.66	1.66	0.42	0.42	0.28	0.28	1.00	1.00	13.89	13.89	17.25	17.25
9.	Jujhari	2.40	2.40	1.50	1.50	0.60	0.60	0.00	0.00	22.24	22.24	26.74	26.74
10.	Khandiguda	2.40	2.40	1.50	1.50	0.60	0.60	0.00	0.00	22.24	22.24	26.74	26.74
11.	Lodijodi	2.40	2.40	1.50	1.50	0.60	0.60	0.00	0.00	22.24	22.24	26.74	26.74
12.	Jodabandh	2.40	2.40	1.50	1.50	0.60	0.60	0.00	0.00	22.24	22.24	26.74	26.74
13.	Nandanmala	2.40	2.40	1.50	1.50	0.60	0.60	0.00	0.00	22.24	22.24	26.74	26.74
14.	Bodaguda	2.40	2.40	1.50	1.50	0.60	0.60	0.00	0.00	22.24	22.24	26.74	26.74
15.	Atalguda	2.40	2.40	1.50	1:50	0.60	0.60	0.00	0.00	22.24	22.24	26.74	26.74
16.	Majhiguda	2.40	2.40	1.50	1.50	0.60	0.60	0.00	0.00	22.24	22.24	26.74	26.74
17.	Marbaiguda	2.40	2.40	1.50	1.50	0.60	0.60	0.00	0.00	22.24	22.24	26.74	26.74
18.	Maligaon	2.40	2.40	1.50	1.50	0.60	0.60	0.00	0.00	22.24	22.24	26.74	26.74
19.	Bandikar	2.40	2.40	1.50	1.50	0.60	0.60	0.00	0.00	22.24	22.24	26.74	26.74
20.	Timajhola	1.73	1.57	0.92	0.92	0.45	0.15	1.00	1.00	15.00	15.46	19.10	19.10
	Total	**46.59**	**46.43**	**28.34**	**28.34**	**11.53**	**11.23**	**2.00**	**2.00**	**431.63**	**432.09**	**520.09**	**520.09**

* The area treated was lesser than other watersheds.

Source: District Rural Development Agency, Koraput, 2009.

The maximum amount of ₹ 432.09 lakh has been spent on the various labour intensive works component, ₹ 2.00 lakh for various entry point activities, for the training purpose ₹ 11.23 lakh, and ₹ 46.43 lakh for the administrative purpose has been spent in all the 20 watershed projects selected for the purpose.

The Entry Point Activity (EPA) is a confidence building measure among the watershed villages of the area before the watershed project starts. The EPA component was there in the EAS watersheds but not in ACA watersheds.

In the watershed projects various training programmes like training of SHGs on savings mobilization, prevention of malaria, integrated pest management on vegetable crops, off season vegetable cultivation, vermi-compost preparation, pisciculture, mushroom cultivation, bee keeping, wheat and sunflower cultivation, etc. are given to stakeholders. In the capacity building measure training on accounting procedure was also given.

The expenditure on administration head includes the preparation of project report, remuneration to community organizer, secretary watershed committee and volunteers, office stationery for PIA office and furniture, etc.

The works which are the major component of the watershed project includes soil and moisture conservation works, water conservation activities, irrigation, plantation/afforestation, livelihood support, etc. About 83 per cent of the total budget for the watershed projects has been spent on this head. Various soil and moisture conservation works like the gully control structure, run-off management structure, land development for water conservation, excavation of tank, earthen check dam, water harvesting structures, mixed tree plantation, cashew plantation, banana cultivation, vegetable cultivation, nursery preparation, vermi-compost preparation, etc. are included besides soil stabilization and ecological restoration. The people of the watershed area get sufficient wage employment during the implementation of the project under this head. The percentage share of various components of the sample watershed projects is given in Figure 5.1.

Demographic Structure of the Sample Households

The total population of the 300 sample households taken as sample selected from 20 watershed area of five blocks of Koraput district is 1,604. The average family size of the sample study came to 5.34. Out of 1,604 persons in the sample households, 797 were male and rest 807

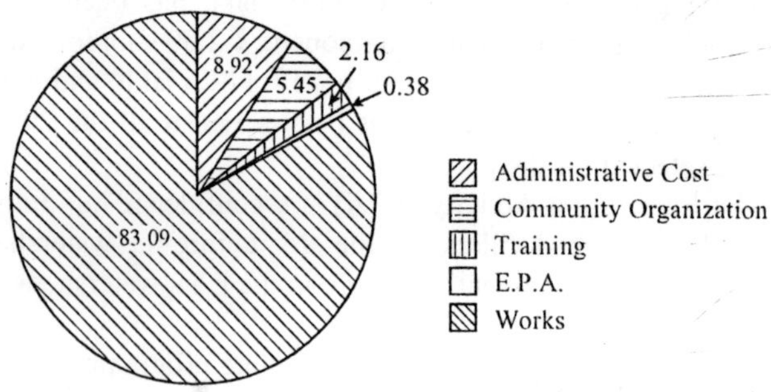

Figure 5.1: Component-wise Expenditure of WDP in Percentage

were female which implied that the sex ratio was in favour of the female. The sex ratio for the sample study area comes to 1,013 females per every 1,000 males which is better than the district average of 999 females per 1,000 males. In the sample, the Scheduled Tribe population is 1,161 which is 72.37 per cent of the total population and the Scheduled Caste population is 132 which is 8.24 per cent of the total population. The rest 311 (19.38%) belong to other castes. The detailed demographic structure of the sample household is given in Table 5.4. In the total population the number of children in the age group (0-7) is 201, they are excluded from the total population while calculating the literacy figure as per the guidelines of 2001 census. In the sample population, it is found that 692 persons (49.32%) are literate and 711 (50.67%) are illiterates. The watershed-wise detail of literacy status is given in Table 5.5. It is found from Table 5.5 that the Malkarbandh watershed of Pottangi block has the highest literacy rate of 73.52 and Pomi watershed of Semiliguda block has the lowest literacy rate of 17.64 per cent.

Farmers' Classification

The classification of farming households according to the area of land under cultivation is given in Table 5.6. Out of the 300 sample households 18 (6%) households are found to be landless, 148 (49.33%) are marginal farmers having up to 1 hectare of land, 80 (26.6%) households belongs to small farmers category having on an average more than 1 hectare but less than 2 hectares of land, 53 (17.67%) households belongs to medium farmers having more than 2 hectares but less than 10 hectares of land and only one household is a large farmer having more than 10 hectares

Table 5.4: Demographic Structure of Sample Households of Koraput District

Sl.No.	Name of the Watershed	ST		SC		Others		Total		Grand Total
		Male	Female	Male	Female	Male	Female	Male	Female	
1.	Panasput	45	46	0	0	0	0	45	46	91
2.	Kankadambo	18	16	2	2	23	27	43	45	88
3.	Ranikana	32	35	0	0	4	4	36	39	75
4.	Pomi	29	37	0	0	0	0	29	37	66
5.	Badaliguda	31	42	0	0	0	0	31	42	73
6.	Badapadu	38	44	0	0	0	0	38	44	82
7.	Girliguda	12	12	0	0	28	25	40	37	77
8.	Malkarbandh	39	38	0	0	3	1	42	39	81
9.	Jujhari	35	38	2	2	7	7	44	47	91
10.	Khandiguda	14	12	2	1	23	25	39	38	77
11.	Lodijodi	28	29	0	0	15	18	43	47	90
12.	Jodabandh	30	34	0	0	10	18	40	52	92
13.	Nandanmala	28	25	9	8	0	0	37	33	70
14.	Bodaguda	23	18	8	9	11	11	42	38	80
15.	Atalguda	15	17	30	27	0	0	45	44	89
16.	Majhiguda	22	18	0	0	14	23	36	41	77
17.	Marbaiguda	25	14	10	8	5	5	40	27	67
18.	Maligaon	39	36	3	2	0	0	42	38	80
19.	Bandikar	38	36	4	3	0	0	42	39	81
20.	Timajhola	41	32	0	0	2	0	43	34	77
	Total	**582**	**579**	**70**	**62**	**145**	**166**	**797**	**807**	**1,604**
	Percentage	**36.28**	**36.09**	**4.37**	**3.8**	**9.03**	**10.34**	**49.69**	**50.31**	**100**

Source: Household Survey, 2008-09.

Table 5.5: Literacy Status of Sample Households of Koraput District

Sl.No.	*Name of Watershed*	*Total Population*	*Literates**	*%*	*Illiterates*	*%*
1.	Panasput	91	36	45.00	44	55.00
2.	Kankadambo	88	41	50.61	40	49.38
3.	Ranikana	75	34	54.83	28	45.16
4.	Pomi	66	9	17.64	42	82.35
5.	Badaliguda	73	26	40.62	38	59.37
6.	Badapadu	82	37	51.38	35	48.61
7.	Girliguda	77	34	51.51	32	48.48
8.	Malkarbandh	81	50	73.52	18	26.47
9.	Jujhari	91	54	71.05	22	28.94
10.	Khandiguda	77	44	57.14	27	42.86
11.	Lodijodi	90	36	40.44	53	59.55
12.	Jodabandh	92	37	45.67	44	54.32
13.	Nandanmala	70	23	37.09	39	62.90
14.	Bodaguda	80	42	60.00	28	40.00
15.	Atalguda	89	29	36.70	50	63.29
16.	Majhiguda	77	30	48.38	32	51.61
17.	Marbaiguda	67	25	45.45	30	54.54
18.	Maligaon	80	35	47.94	38	52.05
19.	Bandikar	81	38	52.05	35	47.94
20.	Timajhola	77	32	47.05	36	52.94
	Total	**1,604**	**692**	**49.33**	**711**	**50.67**

* Children in the age group 0-7 are excluded.

Source: Household Survey, 2008-09.

of land. In Figure 5.2, the percentage distribution of land ownership among sample households is presented.

Table 5.6: Classification of Farmers' Households in the Sample Watersheds under Study

Sl. No.	*Name of the Watershed*	*No. of Landless*	*Marginal Farmers*	*Small Farmers*	*Medium Farmers*	*Large Farmers*
1.	Panasput	3	9	2	1	0
2.	Kankadambo	2	9	2	2	0
3.	Ranikana	1	6	3	5	0
4.	Pomi	1	14	0	0	0
5.	Badaliguda	0	9	5	1	0
6.	Badapadu	1	11	1	2	0
7.	Girliguda	1	9	5	0	0
8.	Malkarbandh	3	9	3	0	0
9.	Jujhari	0	7	3	5	0
10.	Khandiguda	0	13	2	0	0
11.	Lodijodi	0	2	7	6	0
12.	Jodabandh	0	4	8	3	0
13.	Nandanmala	1	6	3	5	0
14.	Bodaguda	0	4	4	7	0
15.	Atalguda	1	6	5	3	0
16.	Majhiguda	0	5	6	4	0
17.	Marbaiguda	2	7	5	1	0
18.	Maligaon	1	7	5	2	0
19.	Bandikar	1	3	8	3	0
20.	Timajhola	0	8	3	3	1
	Total	**18**	**148**	**80**	**53**	**1**
	Percentage	**6**	**49.33**	**26.67**	**17.67**	**0.33**

Source: Household Survey 2008-09.

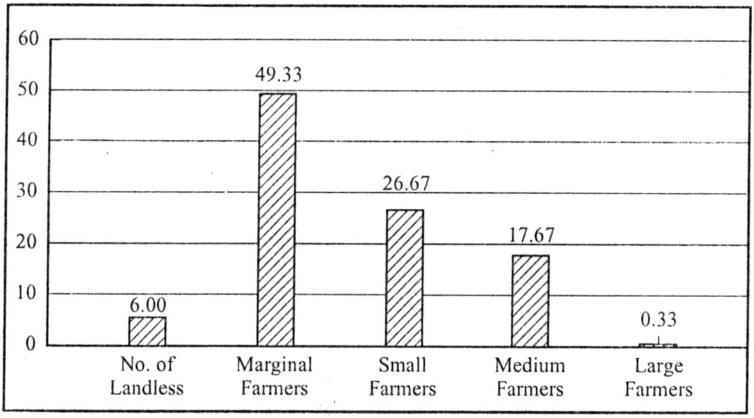

Figure 5.2: Farmers' Classification of Sample Households in Percentage

All these go to show that marginal and small farmers constitute 76 per cent of the total household in the sample. In addition to them there are 6 per cent households who are landless people. Hence, 82 per cent of the households are either small and marginal farmers or landless labourers. It may be mentioned here that the above mentioned classification of land is based on the possession of land with records of rights (ROR). Apart from the cultivation of *patta* land in most part of the district the cultivators also more or less adopt *podu* or shifting cultivation either on the hills or hill slopes.

Work Participation Among Sample Population

Main occupation of a household is that in which a family works for at least for a period of six months or more and they are called main workers. Subsidiary occupation is that in which a person devotes some time of the year in addition to the main occupation and which is less than six months, such a worker is called as marginal worker. Off season activity are taken up by the farmers during their non-farming period to supplement their income. As most of the area under study is rainfed, multiple cropping is not possible in all these areas. Agriculture is mostly subsistence in nature and food security is not 100 per cent achieved. The small and marginal farmers of this area and also landless persons supply their labour for various Government sponsored programmes like NFFWP, MGNREGS, soil conservation works and various works taken up by the watershed projects in the area to supplement their income.

From among the sample (300) households 87 per cent of them have agriculture (cultivation) as their main occupation. Labour is the main

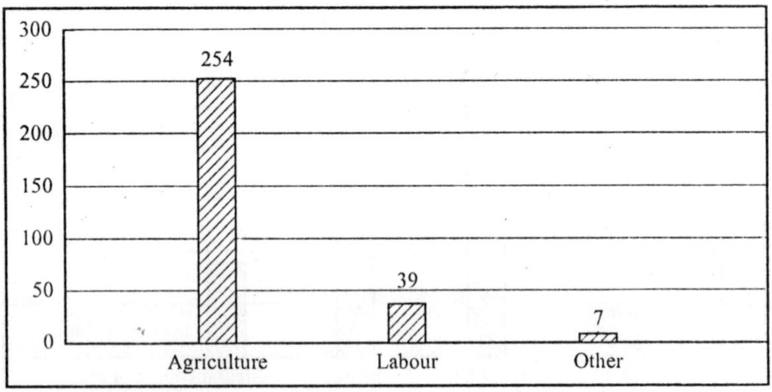

Source: Household Survey 2008-09.

Figure 5.3: Main Occupation of the Sample Households

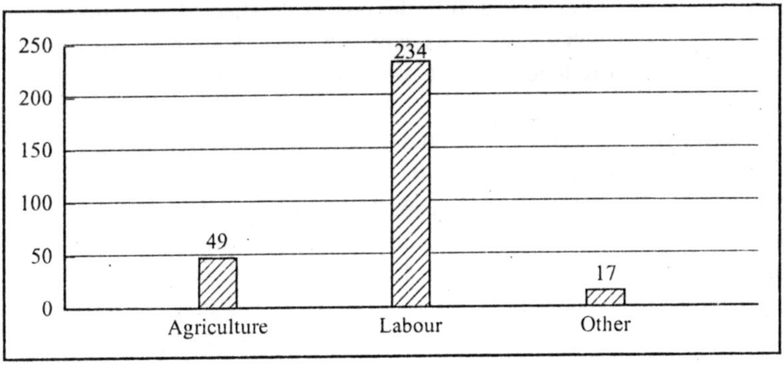

Source: Household Survey 2008-09.

Figure 5.4: Subsidiary Occupation of Sample Households

occupation of only 39 households that is 12.33 per cent and 7 households depend on other occupations other than the above two occupations like business, service and others.

The subsidiary occupation of 49 households is agriculture, 234 households is labour and the rest 17 households is other than agriculture and labour. It is evident from the above figures that vast majority of the people (84.66%) depend on agriculture as their primary source of living.

The Land Use Pattern of Sample Households

The land use pattern of the households in sample study area during the pre- and post-watershed period is given in Table 5.7.

Table 5.7: Land Use Pattern of Sample Households in Pre- and Post-watershed Period *(in acres)*

Sl.No.	*Area (in acres)*	*Pre-W/S**	*% of Total*	*Post-W/S***	*% of Total*
1.	Total Area	1,018.12	100.00	1,064.44	100.00
2.	Irrigated	318.70	31.30	499.90	46.96
3.	Non-Irrigated	663.17	65.13	550.04	51.67
4.	Wasteland	36.25	3.56	14.50	1.36

* Pre-watershed, ** Post-watershed.

Source: Household Survey 2008-09.

It is revealed from Table 5.7 that the irrigated area has increased from 318.70 acres in pre-watershed period to 499.90 acres in post-watershed period, which implies that there is an increase in irrigation potential in the sample area from 31 per cent in pre-watershed to 47 per cent in post-watershed. The non-irrigated area has been reduced from

65 per cent to 52 per cent during the post-watershed period. Similarly, the wasteland which was 3.56 per cent of the total land in pre-watershed period has been reduced to 1.36 per cent of the total area during the post-watershed period.

It has also been observed in the sample study that multiple cropping which means using the land for more than once for agricultural production purposes has been increased from 136 numbers of farmers in pre-watershed period to 225 numbers of farmers in post-watershed period. In the pre-watershed period only 49 per cent of the total farmers were cultivating their land more than once but in post-watershed period the percentage of multiple croppers have increased to 82 per cent of the total farmers in the sample watershed area. The farmers in the study area of Koraput district grow at least one cereal crop in a year for their own consumption and in the irrigated lands during the *kharif* season they may grow some non-paddy crops like vegetables and pulses. The detail of land use pattern of the sample watershed area has been given in Table 5.8. A comparative figure of the land use pattern in pre- and post-watershed period is given in Figure 5.5.

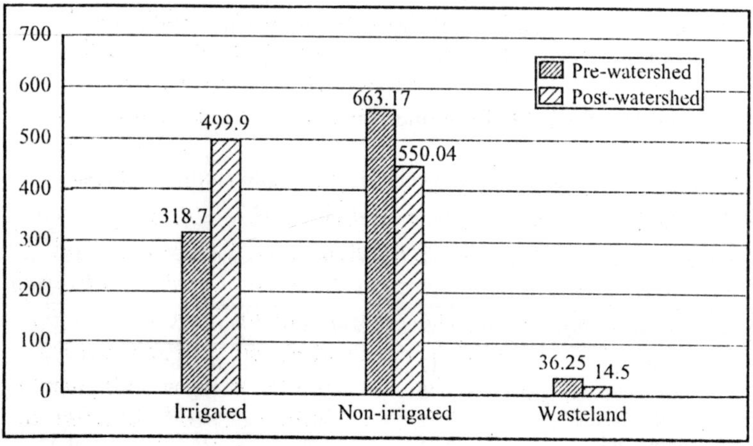

Figure 5.5: Land Use Pattern in Pre- and Post-watershed Period (*in acres*)

Agriculture

This is the most important activity among the sample households on which about 85 per cent of the total household depend upon as their primary source of living. It has been opined that most of the farmers of the study area are subsistence farmers engaged particularly in cereal

Table 5.8: Land Use Pattern of Sample Households under Study Area

(*Post-watershed*)

Sl.No.	*Name of Watershed*	*Total Area (in acres)*	*Irrigated Land (in acres)*	*Non-Irrigated Land (in acres)*	*Wasteland (in acres)*	*Single Crop (No. of families)*	*Multiple Crops (No. of families)*
1.	Panasput	36.77	10.21	26.06	0.50	2	10
2.	Kankadambo	37.00	25.50	11.50	0.00	0	14
3.	Ranikana	107.60	36.50	61.10	10.00	1	12
4.	Pomi	20.95	12.30	8.65	0.00	1	13
5.	Badaliguda	38.50	19.00	19.50	0.00	0	15
6.	Badapadu	39.95	20.75	19.20	0.00	0	14
7.	Girliguda	35.50	13.00	22.50	0.00	0	14
8.	Malkarbandh	25.50	11.80	13.70	0.00	2	12
9.	Jujhari	77.62	38.02	39.60	0.00	4	10
10.	Khandiguda	28.90	20.00	8.90	0.00	7	8
11.	Lodijodi	86.28	25.25	61.03	0.00	5	9
12.	Jodabandh	76.80	36.80	40.00	0.00	3	11
13.	Nandanmala	55.40	29.10	26.30	0.00	4	10
14.	Bodaguda	78.00	36.00	42.00	0.00	6	8
15.	Atalguda	55.00	26.50	28.50	0.00	2	12
16.	Majhiguda	64.50	27.00	35.50	2.00	5	9
17.	Marbaiguda	37.70	19.75	17.95	0.00	3	11
18.	Maligaon	46.70	27.45	17.25	2.00	1	13
19.	Bandikar	57.25	32.80	24.45	0.00	5	9
20.	Timajhola	58.52	32.17	26.35	0.00	2	11
	Total	**1,064.44**	**499.90**	**550.04**	**14.50**	**53**	**225**
	Percentage of Total	**100**	**46.97**	**51.67**	**1.36**	**17.66**	**75**

Source: Household Survey 2008-09.

production. It is further reported by the farmers that there has been a diversification of crops during the post-watershed period on account of availability of irrigation, high yielding varieties of seeds and fertilizers to them. It is also found that in case of most of the crops the per hectare yield has been increased as compared to the pre-project period. A comparative figure of the per hectare yield of important crops of the area in pre- and post-watershed period is given in Table 5.9. The diversification of crops from paddy to non-paddy crops like turmeric, sugarcane, cabbage, cauliflower, tomato, brinjal, carrot, cucumber, ginger, banana, onion, etc. has become possible mainly for the availability of water and other supporting inputs. The role of line departments of Government in providing training, supply of seeds and other inputs to the farmers are responsible for the growth in the productivity of various crops. The formation of Self-Help Groups (SHGs) in recent times and their bank linkages have made the flow of funds easier for the farmers.

Table 5.9: Average Yield of Major Crops in Study Area of Koraput (*Kg/Ha*)

Sl.No.	*Crops*	*Pre-watershed*	*Post-watershed*	*% Change in Production*
1.	Rice	920	1,645	(+) 78.80
2.	Ragi	256	287	(+) 12.10
3.	Niger	360	375	(+) 4.16
4.	Maize	670	762	(+) 13.73
5.	Dal	764	972	(+) 27.22
6.	Kating	187	512	(+) 173.79
7.	Green gram	487	650	(+) 33.47
8.	Potato	470	728	(+) 54.89
9.	Tomato	645	760	(+) 17.82
10.	Carrot*	0	745	(+) 100.00
11.	Ginger*	0	870	(+) 100.00
12.	Cauliflower*	0	1,567	(+) 100.00
13.	Cabbage	312	1,060	(+) 239.74
14.	Papaya	673	1,342	(+) 99.40
15.	Radish	460	736	(+) 60.00
16.	Beans	260	475	(+) 82.69
17.	Brinjal	975	1,475	(+) 51.28
18.	Onion*	0	743	(+) 100.00
19.	Cucumber	376	728	(+) 93.61
20.	Chilli	278	456	(+) 64.02

* Crops which were not produced during pre-Watershed period.
Source: Household Survey, 2008-09.

It was found during the field study that the contribution of Mali community is significant in producing various types of vegetables in this region. The Malis are expert in vegetable cultivation. The Mali community produce Cabbage, Cucumber, Onion, Carrot, Cauliflower, Tamato, Potato, Radish, Ginger apart from the cereals and pulses. In course of our visit to various sample villages, we noticed the locations where the Mali community predominantly reside and found that they have utilized their land to its maximum extent. Some of the crops it was confessed, which were not produced in this locality a few years ago are now being produced by the local farmers. It could be possible mainly on account of availability of water for irrigation and other facilities through watershed projects. In Figure 5.6 the comparative figures for pre- and post-watershed period yield of major crops of the sample study area is presented.

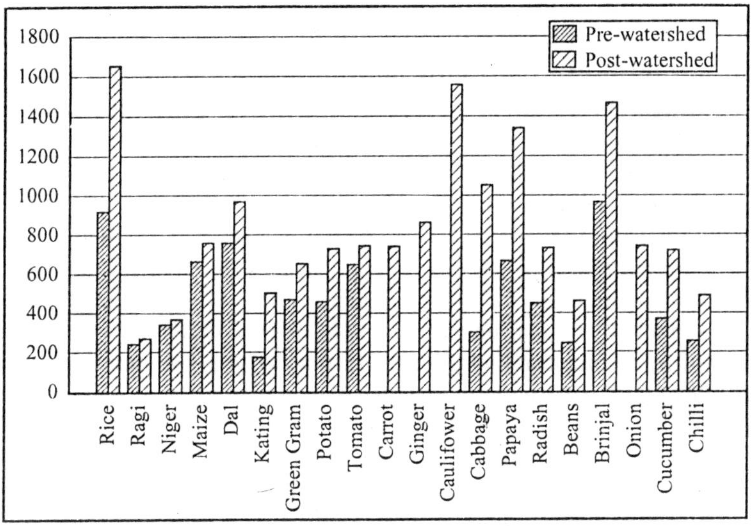

Figure 5.6: Average Yield of Various Agricultural Commodities in Pre- and Post-Watershed Period (kg/ha)

In Figure 5.6, the yield of various important crops in the pre- and post-watershed development projects is shown. It can be seen from the above figure that some of the crops like carrot, ginger, cauliflower, onion, etc. which were not produced during the pre-watershed period are being produced after the watershed programme was implemented. At the same time there has been a substantial increase in production of Cabbage (240%), Kating (174%), Papaya (99%), Rice (79%) and in some other crops there has been only a moderate increase over this period. In case of niger there has been the least increase in production over this period (4.16%). It is found that the productivity of various crops varies from place to place in the study area depending on several factors which includes the availability of irrigation facility, use of fertilizers and pesticides, use of HYV seeds, etc. The share of agriculture in the total income of the households has been increased from 18 per cent in pre-watershed to 23 per cent in post-watershed project, the details of which is given in Table 5.9.

The cropping intensity of the sample area which was 122 per cent in pre-watershed period has increased to 176 per cent in post-watershed period. The higher cropping intensity means that a higher portion of the net area is being cropped more than once during one agricultural year.

Livestock

The livestock plays an important role as it provides them drought animals to be used in cultivation and supplements their dietary deficiencies and increase in income. In the study area of Koraput district the major livestock are the cattle, Buffalo, Goat, Sheep, poultry and pigs. The tribal people generally use these animals for agricultural activities or for consumption purposes rather than for commercial purposes. The cattle and buffaloes are mostly used as drought animals for cultivating their fields and generally not for milk as some of the tribal communities have a taboo to mulch the cattle. The goats and sheep are used mainly for consumption purposes and are sold in the market in case of some financial emergency. The rearing of poultry by the rural people of this area is almost universal. They use it for eggs, chicken and sometimes sell it in the market to get some money, to overcome their financial problems. Pigs are generally reared by the lower caste people like the rellis of this area and it is consumed by them only.

The people of the study area do not rear the livestock exclusively for commercial purposes. The animals and birds reared by these people are mostly local varieties. The use of hybrid varieties of animals and birds is very rare. The researcher could find only one farmer of Laxmipur block belonging to general category, rearing hybrid variety of cattle and managing a dairy farm with eight cows for commercial purpose. The respondents say that the high yielding cows and buffaloes are not surviving in the local conditions due to non-availability of proper feed and vaccination. The high yielding varieties of poultry like Banaraj which was provided by the veterinary departments in the convergence scheme are hard to find after a period of time. The livestock population in pre- and post-watershed is provided in Table 5.10. A comparative

Table 5.10: Livestock Population in Pre- and Post-watershed Period in the Sample Watershed Village of Koraput District

Sl.No.	Name of Watershed	Cattle		Buffalo		Goat/Sheep		Poultry		Pigs	
		Pre-w/s	Post-w/s	Pre-w/s	Post-w/s	Pre-w/s	Post-w/s	Pre-w/s	Post-w/s	Pre-w/s	Post-w/s
1.	Panasput	189	237	28	36	245	353	126	188	49	67
2.	Kankadambo	289	312	17	22	114	131	85	162	17	12
3.	Ranikana	167	225	107	138	317	596	377	559	0	0
4.	Pomi	203	278	179	223	191	250	108	205	27	38
5.	Badaliguda	63	129	0	0	47	93	319	437	32	21
6.	Badapadu	227	341	21	19	217	319	267	310	21	31
7.	Girliguda	347	572	179	226	393	512	159	187	0	0
8.	Malkarbandh	56	44	11	7	27	34	147	155	27	35
9.	Jujhari	217	263	19	33	79	112	73	198	9	20
10.	Khandiguda	179	344	72	100	178	232	285	289	32	23
11.	Lodijodi	177	231	21	28	121	197	64	108	12	15
12.	Jodabandh	292	482	27	36	107	181	384	578	21	39
13.	Nandanmala	647	957	164	132	417	546	470	898	27	21
14.	Bodaguda	1,009	1,217	81	125	317	658	795	1,272	31	23
15.	Atalguda	847	1,345	107	132	529	641	844	1,195	0	10
16.	Majhiguda	1,018	1,640	75	120	479	701	630	1,192	9	20
17.	Marbaiguda	78	136	19	23	42	61	290	350	0	0
18.	Maligaon	103	125	17	21	27	63	131	250	0	0
19.	Bandikar	220	249	27	42	79	138	289	526	32	45
20.	Timajhola	117	240	119	135	276	435	378	415	107	130
	Total	**6,445**	**9,367**	**1,290**	**1,598**	**4,202**	**6,253**	**6,221**	**9,474**	**453**	**550**
	% increase		**45.34**		**23.88**		**48.81**		**52.29**		**21.41**

Source: Household Survey, 2008-09.

figure of the livestock population in pre- and post-watershed period is shown in Figure 5.7.

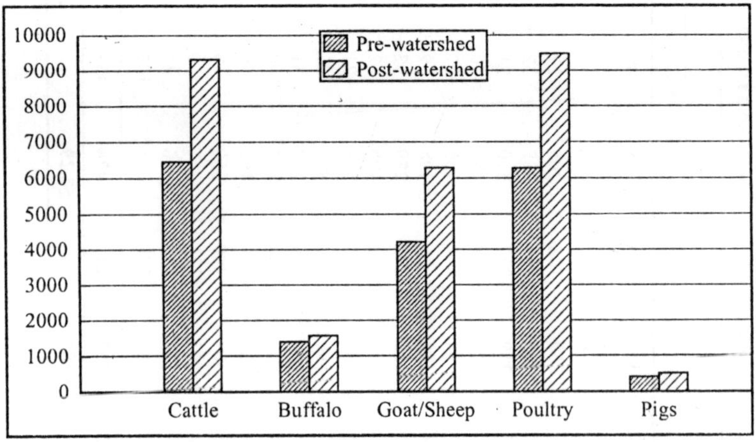

Figure 5.7: Livestock Population in Pre- and Post-watershed Period (in Nos.)

From Table 5.10 and Figure 5.7, it is clear that total number of various animals and birds during the post-watershed period have registered a growth over the pre-watershed period. The highest growth has been registered by poultry population which has increased from 6,221 in pre-w/s period to 9,474 in post-watershed period, i.e. 52.29 per cent growth in its population. Next to poultry the population of goat/ sheep has increased from 4202 in pre-w/s period to 6253 in the post-w/s period, i.e. a growth of 48.81 per cent over the period. The cattle population too has been increased during this period from 6,445 to 9,367 (a growth of 45.32%). The population of buffalo has also increased by about 24 per cent during this period and the least increase in population in this period is the pig's population which has registered only 21 per cent growth over the period. The number of pigs has increased from 453 in pre-w/s period to 550 in post-w/s period. The growth of livestock population in the post-watershed period may be ascribed to the better availability of fodder and water after the implementation of WDPs. During this period, the increase in irrigation facility has contributed to an increase in the fodder for the livestock. In the study area the people leave the cattle, buffalo, goat, sheep, pigs and poultry for grazing during the day time and they never feed these animals anything purchased from the market. Figure 5.8 shows the per cent share of income from various items.

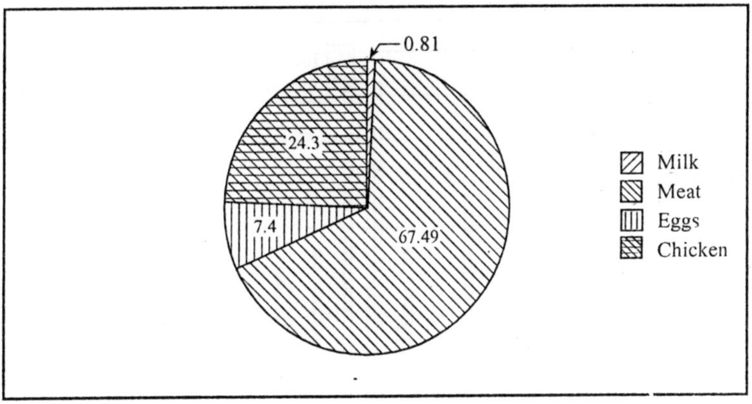

Figure 5.8: Share of Income from Livestock in Post-watershed (%)

Non-Timber Forest Products (NTFPs)

The tribal and other rural people of Koraput are intimately linked with the forest. Forest is almost everything for a tribal's survival. But due to gradual decline in the forest cover over a period of time these forest dependent people are finding it hard to eke out their living. These tribal people used to collect various roots, fruits, leaves and flowers for food, firewood, agricultural implements, housing materials, medicinal herbs, drinks and fodder, etc. from the forest. The non-timber forest products are usually collected from the nearby jungles by the villagers. A few years ago, when there was dense forest cover in the locality there was no difficulty for these people to collect various NTFPs and use it for their own consumption or to sell it in the market to supplement their income. It is found through household survey that the share of NTFPs in the total income of the sample household has declined considerably over the period. It was reported by the respondents that in some areas, the villagers no more go to the forest to collect the NTFPs except the firewood. It is also found from the survey that the NTFPs are also not sufficiently available in the study area of the district. The households in most parts use the NTFPs collected for their own consumption and not for sale in the market. The availability of alternative sources of income like the agriculture and wage employment in the watershed area has also discouraged the NTFP collection and its sale in the market. The comparative figure of the income from NTFPs during the pre- and post-watershed period is given in Figure 5.9.

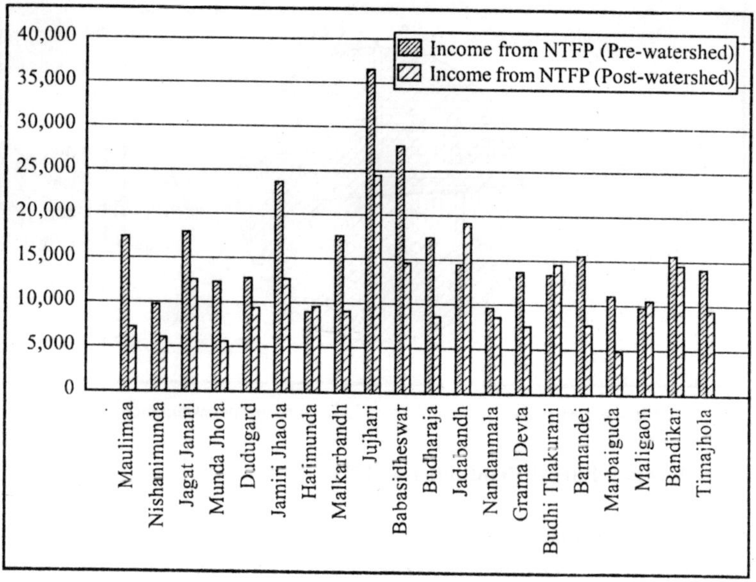

Figure 5.9: Income from NTFP in Pre- and Post-watershed Period

It is clear from Figure 5.9 that the income from non-timber forest products has declined in all except four watersheds. There is only marginal increase in the income of these four watersheds over the period. The main items of NTFP in the study area is that of firewood, broom, various roots, fruits, honey, medicinal plants, etc. The share of income from NTFPs to the total income has been reduced from 5.12 per cent in pre-watershed period to only 1.71 per cent in post-watershed period. It is important to note that the total income from NTFP of all the sample watershed taken together was ₹ 3,16,030 in pre-watershed period has been reduced to ₹ 2,06,521 in the post-watershed period. The reasons for the decline in share of NTFPs in the total income are many. Some of the important reasons are:

(i) The man day's income from NTFP is much less as compared to the man days wage in government wage employment programmes which discourages the villagers to collect and sale NTFP in the market.

(ii) Engagement in agricultural activities for most part of the year on account of availability of irrigation facility through the watershed projects.

(iii) Availability of more wage employment opportunities than before on account of various Government sponsored programmes.

Income of the Sample Households from Various Sources

In the sample survey, information was collected from the households in the watershed area about their income received from various sources. A comparative statement of the income received in pre- and post-watershed period has been prepared by compiling the various income sources. It is found that the main sources of income of the sample households are the income from agriculture, wage employment, livestock and non-timber forest produce, etc. The other sources of income include the income from small business, service, contractors, etc. The detail of the income from various sources during the pre- and post-watersheds has been given in Tables 5.11 and 5.12. The major source of income both in pre- and post-watershed period goes to labour or wage employment. Even though the share of labour in total income of the household has reduced from 61 per cent in pre-watershed period to 53 per cent in post-watershed period, in absolute terms the income from labour as a source of income has increased from ₹ 37,70,497.00 in pre-watershed period to ₹ 63,96,760 in the post-watershed period. The opportunity for the households to earn more through the labour engagement has increased during the watershed project period and after its completion. A number of labour intensive programmes by the Government like the Employment Assurance Scheme (EAS), National Food for Work Programme (NFFWP), Soil conservation works at the village level, watershed project works and in recent times the Mahatma Gandhi National Rural Employment Guarantee Scheme (MGNREGS) has increased the opportunity for the rural people for earning through wage employment in the agricultural off season period.

In Tables 5.11 and 5.12 and Figures 5.10, 5.11 and 5.12, the comparative share of income from various sources in the pre- and post-watershed period is given. The share of agriculture in the total income has been increased from 18.22 per cent in pre-watershed period to 22.99 per cent in post-watershed period. The share of livestock has also marginally increased from 10.39 per cent to 12.27 per cent during the same period. The share of NTFPs in the total income of the sample households has declined in the post-watershed period as compared to pre-watershed period. The share of NTFPs was 5.12 per cent in pre-watershed period which has declined to 1.71 per cent in post-watershed period. It is because of the fact that the inhabitants in the Watershed areas spend more time in agriculture and other related activities, and

Table 5.11: Income of Sample Households from All Sources (*Pre-w/s*)

Sl.No.	*Name of the Watershed*	*Agriculture*	*Livestock*	*NTFP*	*Labour*	*Others*	*Total*
1.	Panasput	53,156	35,105	17,400	1,96,300	7,000.00	3,08,961
2.	Kankadambo	82,124	67,000	9,700	2,21,412	21,900.00	4,02,136
3.	Ranikana	64,645	46,000	18,000	2,10,805	16,800.00	3,56,250
4.	Pomi	34,975	21,300	11,750	1,57,310	Nil	2,25,335
5.	Badaliguda	36,109	14,500	12,620	1,83,100	13,500.00	2,59,829
6.	Badapadu	65,155	12,100	22,700	2,03,100	9,800.00	3,12,855
7.	Girliguda	37,605	29,115	8,650	1,06,700	6,500.00	1,88,570
8.	Malkarbandh	32,915	14,150	17,250	1,21,500	12,150.00	1,97,965
9.	Jujhari	81,600	21,200	36,500	2,88,300	39,500.00	4,67,100
10.	Khandiguda	74,300	28,700	27,510	1,23,000	24,000.00	2,77,510
11.	Lodijodi	50,605	32,600	17,200	1,90,200	21,300.00	3,11,905
12.	Jodabandh	41,700	19,300	14,100	1,49,000	Nil	2,24,100
13.	Nandanmala	66,200	45,100	9,300	2,00,000	16,500.00	3,37,100
14.	Bodaguda	43,000	54,500	13,500	1,60,700	18,200.00	2,89,900
15.	Atalguda	74,200	29,600	12,600	2,83,000	22,000.00	4,21,400
16.	Majhiguda	36,250	38,500	16,150	1,94,600	14,000.00	2,99,500
17.	Marbaiguda	73,000	42,100	11,650	2,21,170	11,200.00	3,59,120
18.	Maligaon	64,400	20,200	9,650	2,12,000	22,500.00	3,28,750
19.	Bandikar	58,115	22,100	16,100	2,36,200	18,000.00	3,50,515
20.	Timajhola	53,206	47,000	13,700	1,12,100	21,200.00	2,47,206
Total Amount		**11,23,260**	**6,40,170**	**3,16,030**	**37,70,497**	**3,16,050**	**61,66,007**
Percentage		**18.22**	**10.39**	**5.12**	**61.15**	**5.12**	**100.00**

Source: Household Survey 2008-09.

Table 5.12: Income of Sample Households from All Sources (*Post-w/s*)

Sl.No.	*Name of the Watershed*	*Agriculture*	*Livestock*	*NTFP*	*Labour*	*Others*	*Total*
1.	Panasput	103,579	41,156	7,800	271,892	Nil	424,427
2.	Kankadambo	439,982	189,300	6,450	584,834	409,000	1,629,566
3.	Ranikana	349,940	181,810	12,560	508,565	423,659	1,476,534
4.	Pomi	107,420	46,950	6,300	248,645	Nil	409,315
5.	Badaliguda	88,991	28,000	9,150	249,477	11,300	386,918
6.	Badapadu	106,653	101,520	12,180	273,726	44,000	538,079
7.	Girliguda	67,312	34,550	9,627	181,690	19,700	312,879
8.	Malkarbandh	52,547	17,350	8,445	196,838	14,500	289,680
9.	Jujhari	224,431	48,255	24,322	604,692	48,000	949,700
10.	Khandiguda	138,611	62,600	14,640	275,825	21,700	513,376
11.	Lodijodi	87,108	55,250	7,670	294,565	24,115	468,708
12.	Jodabandh	86,970	50,900	19,170	244,050	31,900	432,990
13.	Nandanmala	136,624	102,075	Nil	311,517	28,700	578,916
14.	Bodaguda	86,365	105,700	7,160	276,759	26,140	502,124
15.	Ataiguda	148,220	63,500	14,350	436,238	17,600	679,908
16.	Majhiguda	89,254	89,600	7,127	279,385	16,500	481,866
17.	Marbaiguda	132,407	88,740	5,100	310,901	Nil	537,148
18.	Maligaon	108,393	36,350	11,120	331,957	9,400	497,220
19.	Bandikar	111,162	51,600	14,180	322,894	17,200	517,036
20.	Timajhola	108,964	86,000	9,170	192,310	46,500	442,944
	Total	**27,74,933**	**14,81,206**	**2,06,521**	**6396,760**	**1,209,914**	**12,069,334**
	Percentage of Total	**22.99**	**12.27**	**1.71**	**53**	**10.03**	**100**

Source: Household Survey 2008-09.

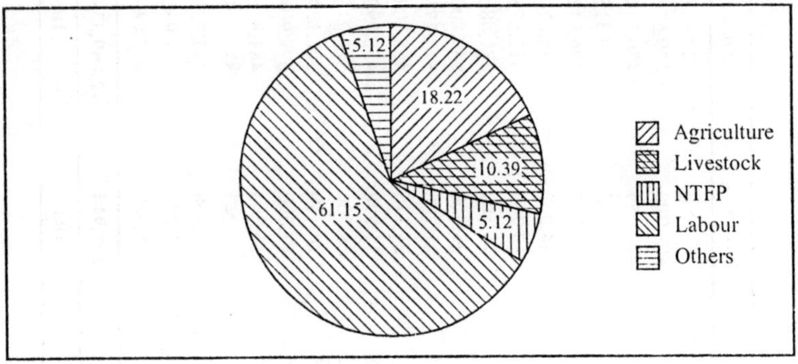

Figure 5.10: Share of Income from Various Sources in Pre-watershed (%)

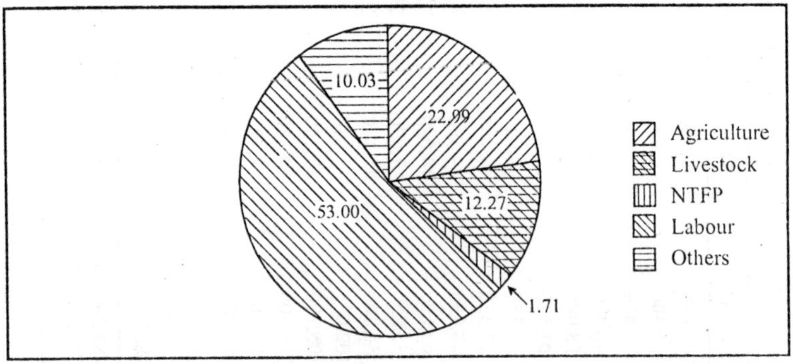

Figure 5.11: Share of Income from Various Sources in Post-watershed (%)

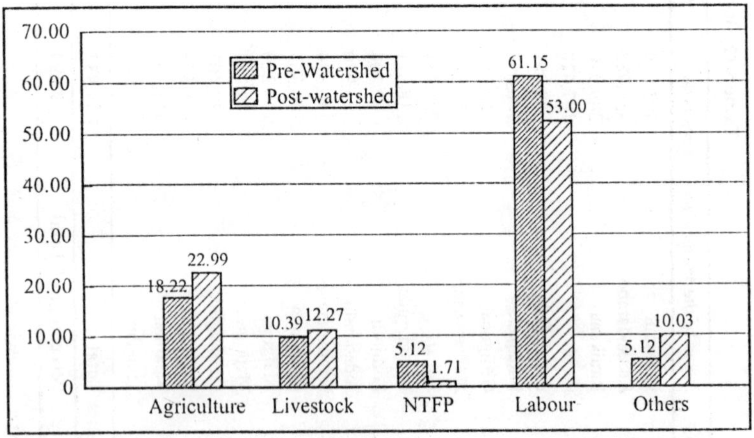

Figure 5.12: Comparative Share of Income from Various Sources in Pre- and Post-watershed (%)

also in wage labour which is presently available under various employment schemes, and spends less time in collection and sale of NTFPs. Whatever, NTFPs they collect; it is mostly used for self-consumption. Similarly, the share of wage income has also declined in the post-watershed period as compared to pre-watershed period. The share of labour income in the total income of the household has declined from 61.15 per cent in pre-watershed period to 53.00 per cent in post-watershed period. Still the contribution of income from wage labour is the highest both in pre- and post-watershed periods. The share of income from other sources which includes the business, services, etc. in the total income of the household has almost doubled in post-watershed period as compared to pre-watershed period. The share of other income was only 5.12 per cent in the pre-watershed period which has been increased to 10.03 per cent of total income in post-watershed period.

An increase of income from agriculture and livestock activities may be ascribed to the boom in the agricultural activity mainly on account of the implementation of the watersheds in these areas. Also the increase in the cropping intensity and use of HYV seeds and other agricultural inputs has contributed to the increase in income of the agricultural sector in the post-watershed period over the pre-watershed period. The increase in the availability of fodder and drinking water in the watershed areas has increased the number of livestock population in these areas.

The total annual income of all the sample households from all sources came to ₹ 61,66,007 in pre-watershed (2002-03) period which has increased in the post-watershed period (2006-07) to ₹ 1,20,69,334. The per capita income in pre-watershed period was only ₹ 3,844.14 and the same during the post-watershed period has gone up to ₹ 7,524.52.

Pattern of Expenditure of the Sample Households

The important expenditures of the households have been broadly categorized under Food, Clothing, Housing, Education, Health, Festivals, Fuel and Others. An attempt was made to collect the amount of expenditure made by the sample households on various items mentioned above through the questionnaires served. The item-wise average annual household expenditure in percentages is given in Table 5.13.

The share of expenditure on food has declined from 52 per cent in pre-watershed to 43 per cent in post-watershed period. However, out of the total household expenditures, the share of food is the highest both in pre- and post-watershed periods, followed by clothing, festivals and housing, etc. On the other hand, the share of expenditure on other non-food items like clothing, housing, education, health, festivals and fuel has increased in post-watershed period in comparison to the pre-watershed period. The percentage share of miscellaneous items coming under the head others has remained constant at 4 per cent in both pre- and post-watershed period.

Table 5.13: Annual Household Expenditure on Various Items (%) in Pre- and Post-watershed

Sl.No.	*Items of Expenditure*	*Pre-Watershed (2002-03)*	*Post-Watershed (2006-07)*
1.	Food	52	43
2.	Clothing	16	18
3.	Housing	7	8
4.	Education	2	3
5.	Health	5	7
6.	Fuel	2	4
7.	Festivals	12	13
8.	Others	4	4
	Total	**100**	**100**

Source: Household Survey 2008-09.

The per capita expenditure of sample households has been calculated from the sample data collected from the individual households. The watershed-wise detail of total expenditure per annum, per capita expenditure per annum and per capita expenditure per month has been given in Table 5.14.

In the pre-watershed period (2002-03) out of the twenty selected watersheds the per capita expenditure per month of Jujhari watershed of Borigumma block was the highest (₹ 349.00) and the Malkarbandh watershed of Pottangi block had the lowest average income of ₹ 115. The total income of all the households per annum was ₹ 42,19,526 in pre-watershed period (2002-03). The same has increased to ₹ 92,49,448 in post-watershed period. The per capita expenditure per annum in pre-watershed period was highest (₹ 4188.00) for Jujhari watershed of Borigumma block and lowest (₹ 1345.00) in Badaliguda watershed of Pottangi block. In the year 2002-03, the average per capita expenditure per annum for all households was ₹ 2,625. In the post-watershed period, the per capita expenditure per month was highest (₹ 17,397) for the Kankadambo watershed of Semiliguda block and lowest (₹ 2,154) for Malkarbandh watershed of Pottangi block.

As per the Report of the Expert Group on Estimation of Poverty (Tendulkar Committee, 2009) of Planning Commission, Government of

Table 5.14: Per Capita Expenditure of Sample Households Population of Koraput District

Sl.No.	*Name of the Watershed*	*Total Expenditure per Annum*		*Per Capita Exp. per Annum*		*Per Capita Exp. per Month*	
		Pre-w/s	*Post-w/s*	*Pre-w/s*	*Post-w/s*	*Pre-w/s*	*Post-w/s*
1.	Panasput	1,36,590	2,56,848	1,501	2,823	124.00	235.00
2.	Kankadambo	2,10,913	15,30,944	2,397	17,397	200.00	1,450.00
3.	Ranikana	1,99,092	12,31,544	2,655	16,421	221.00	1,368.00
4.	Pomi	1,41,708	2,60,084	2,147	3,941	179.00	328.00
5.	Badaliguda	98,160	1,73,642	1,345	2,379	112.00	198.00
6.	Badapadu	1,54,068	2,53,068	1,879	3,086	157.00	257.00
7.	Girliguda	1,43,040	2,07,750	1,858	2,698	155.00	225.00
8.	Malkarbandh	1,12,224	1,74,480	1,385	2,154	115.00	180.00
9.	Jujhari	3,81,120	5,79,700	4,188	6,370	349.00	531.00
10.	Khandiguda	2,43,804	4,13,676	3,166	5,372	264.00	448.00
11.	Lodijodi	2,59,428	4,35,708	2,883	4,841	240.00	403.00
12.	Jodabandh	2,27,045	3,85,692	2,468	4,192	206.00	349.00
13.	Nandanmala	1,76,088	4,36,416	2,516	6,235	210.00	520.00
14.	Bodaguda	2,09,472	4,20,964	2,618	5,262	218.00	439.00
15.	Atalguda	2,56,550	5,51,808	2,883	6,200	240.00	517.00
16.	Majhiguda	2,30,668	4,35,816	2,996	5,660	250.00	472.00
17.	Marbaiguda	2,21,568	3,28,308	3,307	4,900	276.00	400.00
18.	Maligaon	2,68,460	4,21,320	3,356	5,267	280.00	439.00
19.	Bandikar	2,83,800	3,99,036	3,504	4,926	292.00	411.00
20.	Timajhola	2,65,728	3,52,644	3,451	4,580	288.00	382.00

Source: Household Survey, 2008-09.

India, poverty line is determined as a monthly expenditure of ₹ 407.78 for rural areas and ₹ 497.31 for urban areas in Odisha. The base year of calculation of poverty line was 2004. On the basic of this estimation, at the outset, all the sample households in the watershed area on an average lived below the poverty line during the pre-watershed period. In the post-watershed period (2006-07), the average per month expenditure of 10 watersheds is above 408.00. That means the average per month expenditure of sample households of 10 sample watersheds are below the poverty line. It may be mentioned here that the above figures are projected with reference to expert Group estimation of poverty taking 2004-05 as the base year, without making any adjustment taking into account the rate of inflation during these periods. But one thing becomes clear that there has been a positive change in the standard of living of the people living in sample watershed area, as a result of which about 50 per cent of them have crossed the poverty line by post-watershed period.

Food Security of Sample Households

Food security refers to the availability of food and one's access to it. A household is considered as food secure when its occupants do not live in hunger or fear of starvation (Wikipedia). Food insecurity is one of the important issues in the tribal belt of Odisha particularly in the KBK (Koraput-Bolangir-Kalahandi) districts. This area is known for prevalence of hunger and sometimes for the sale of child due to severe poverty and hunger. The food security aspect of the sample households has been projected and analyzed in Table 5.15. Figure 5.13 represents the status of food security in pre- and post-watershed period.

Table 5.15: Food Security of Sample Households in Pre- and Post-Watershed

Sl.No.	*Period*	*Pre-watershed*	*% of Total in Pre-w/s*	*Post-watershed*	*% of Total in Post-w/s*
1.	Up to 3 Months	67	22.33	17	5.67
2.	3-6 Months	146	48.67	104	34.67
3.	6-9 Months	59	19.67	96	32.00
4.	9-12 Months	28	9.33	83	27.66
	Total	**300**	**100**	**300**	**100**

Source: Household Survey 2008-09.

From Table 5.15, it would be seen that in the pre-watershed period only 9.33 per cent of the households were food secured for 12 months or one year, 19.67 per cent were secured up to 9 months, 48.67 per cent of the household were food secured only for a period up to 6 months and 22.33 per cent of the sample household were food secured only for a period of up to 3 months.

In the post-watershed period (2006-07) about 28 per cent of the total households were food secured for the whole year, 32 per cent were secured for up to 9 months, 35 per cent were food secured up to 6 months and the rest 6 per cent were secured only up to 3 months. This shows that there is a positive impact of the implementation of the watershed programmes in a tribal dominated backward district of the state. A comparative analysis of food security in pre- and post-watershed period has been shown in Figure 5.13.

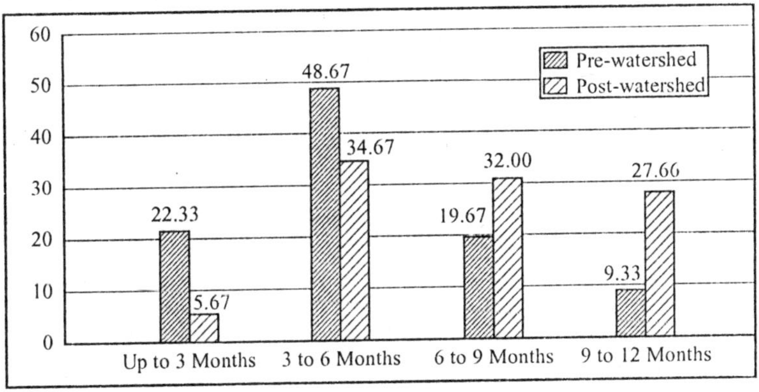

Figure 5.13: Food Security in Pre- and Post-watershed Period (%)

Saving Status of the Sample Households

Data collected from the sample households show that the people in rural areas more or less save money in spite of several adversaries faced by them. A detailed analysis of the saving potential is given in Tables 5.16 and 5.17 for the pre- and post-watershed period respectively. These people save money in Banks, Post offices and Self-Help Groups (SHGs). etc., some people simply keep money with them without saving in Banks or Post offices which amounts to hoarding. It is surprising but true that in the entire 20 watersheds, selected in the sample, there has been not a single bank or post office. The people either keep the money with them, or go to nearby block headquarter to deposit their money in Bank or post offices. There are of course various banks like the Koraput Central Cooperative Bank (KCC Bank), Utkal Gramya Bank (UGB) formerly known as Koraput Panchabati Gramya Bank (KPGB) and Public Sector Banks operating in the block headquarters. The post offices are functioning in some of the Gram Panchayats. The banking habit of the people of the sample watershed area is very poor as they are mostly illiterate, ignorant and not acquainted with the banks. The people of these areas prefer to keep the cash with themselves rather than keeping it in the bank due to non-availability of banking facility at nearby places. The savings status of households during the pre- and post-watershed period is given in Table 5.18.

Table 5.16: Saving Status of Sample Households (Pre-watershed)

Sl.No.	*Name of Watershed*	*Amount Saved (in ₹)*			*Total Amount of Savings*
		Bank	*Post Office/Others*	*Own*	
1.	Panasput	Nil	Nil	6,000	6,000
2.	Kankadambo	6,000	Nil	3,500	9,500
3.	Ranikana	17,000	4,000	6,200	27,200
4.	Pomi	15,300	Nil	12,000	27,300
5.	Badaliguda	Nil	Nil	21,500	21,500
6.	Badapadu	17,000	3,000	22,000	42,000
7.	Girliguda	12,000	Nil	7,500	19,500
8.	Malkarbandh	17,000	Nil	4,000	21,000
9.	Jujhari	Nil	Nil	3,200	3,200
10.	Khandiguda	Nil	Nil	6,000	6,000
11.	Lodijodi	Nil	Nil	7,000	7,000
12.	Jodabandh	6,200	5,000	3,700	14,900
13.	Nandanmala	2,000	Nil	8,500	10,500
14.	Bodaguda	12,500	9,000	7,000	28,500
15.	Atalguda	Nil	Nil	14,000	14,000
16.	Majhiguda	13,000	Nil	11,000	24,000
17.	Marbaiguda	17,500	3,000	8,000	28,500
18.	Maligaon	Nil	Nil	12,000	12,000
19.	Bandikar	Nil	Nil	6,000	6,000
20.	Timajhola	Nil	1,500	6,800	8,300
	Total	**1,35,500**	**25,500**	**1,75,900**	**3,36,900**

Source: Household Survey 2008-09.

The share of bank in mobilizing the total savings has increased from 40.22 per cent in pre-watershed period to 61.42 per cent in post-watershed period. The share of Post Office/others have reduced from 7.57 per cent to 3.1 per cent during this period. Similarly, saving with self has also reduced from 52.21 per cent to 35.42 per cent in the same period. The total saving has increased by ₹ 19,48,100 in post-watershed period

(2006-07) over the pre-watershed period (2002-03). The increase in the savings is because of the increase in the volume of income of the households on account of spread of economic activities and employment of people in them during the operation of watershed projects and till their completion.

Table 5.17: Saving Status of Sample Households (Post-watershed)

Sl.No.	*Name of Watershed*	*Amount Saved (in ₹)*			*Total Amount of Savings*
		Bank	*Post Office/Others*	*Own*	
1.	Panasput	13,200	Nil	58,750	71,950
2.	Kankadambo	2,15,000	Nil	30,000	2,45,000
3.	Ranikana	1,41,000	Nil	31,600	1,72,600
4.	Pomi	72,000	40,000	8,000	1,20,000
5.	Badaliguda	84,000	Nil	71,000	1,55,000
6.	Badapadu	1,50,000	Nil	1,61,000	3,11,000
7.	Girliguda	46,000	Nil	29,500	75,500
8.	Malkarbandh	50,900	Nil	38,000	88,900
9.	Jujhari	1,53,000	Nil	1,61,000	3,14,000
10.	Khandiguda	15,000	17,000	19,700	51,700
11.	Lodijodi	Nil	Nil	11,000	11,000
12.	Jodabandh	27,000	900	30,400	58,300
13.	Nandanmala	86,000	Nil	8,500	94,500
14.	Bodaguda	7,500	Nil	12,800	20,300
15.	Atalguda	34,000	Nil	35,100	69,100
16.	Majhiguda	12,250	Nil	7,500	19,750
17.	Marbaiguda	1,66,800	Nil	6,000	1,72,800
18.	Maligaon	35,200	Nil	19,700	54,900
19.	Bandikar	68,000	Nil	46,000	1,14,000
20.	Timajhola	27,000	14,500	24,000	65,500
	Total	**14,03,850**	**72,400**	**8,09,550**	**22,85,800**
	In percentage	**61.42**	**3.16**	**35.42**	**100**

Source: Household Survey 2008-09.

Table 5.18: Savings with Various Institutions in Pre- and Post-watershed Period

Sl.No.	*Institution*	*Pre-watershed (in ₹)*	*% of Total in Pre-w/s*	*Post-watershed (in ₹)*	*% of Total in Post-w/s*
1.	Bank	1,35,000	40.22	14,03,850	61.42
2.	Post Office/Others*	25,500	7.57	72,400	3.16
3.	Keeping at home	1,75,900	52.21	8,09,550	35.42
	Total	**3,36,900**	**100.00**	**22,85,800**	**100.00**

* Others include Micro-Finance Institutions and SHGs.

Source: Household Survey 2008-09.

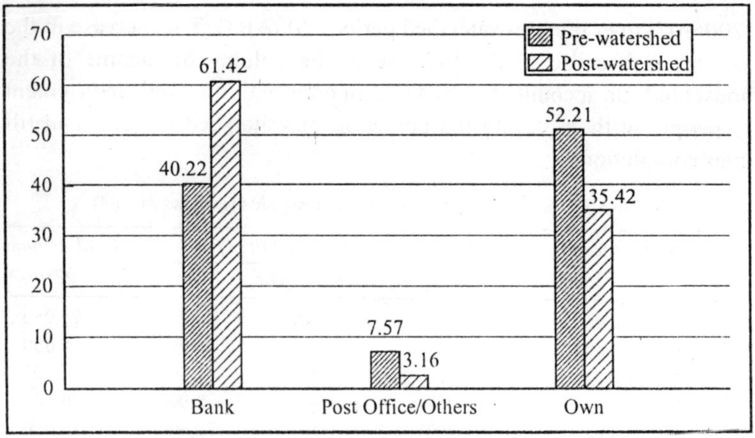

Figure 5.14: Share of Various Institutions in Total Savings in Pre- and Post-watershed Period

Indebtedness Status of Sample Households

The rural and tribal people need credit both for their consumption and production purposes. These people generally face a lot of difficulties in availing loan at the appropriate time. The non-availability of adequate institutional sources of loan has increased the worries of the rural masses of the study area. Sometimes, these people have to depend on moneylenders, relatives and friends in order to meet their emergency financial requirements. The banks and post offices are not always ready to advance loans to these people due to the non-availability of tangible assets to mortgage by the rural farmers. In the household survey conducted watershed-wise sought information on various sources of loan, purpose of loan, amount of repayment and outstanding loan amount. The rate of interest on the loan amount varies between 7 per cent and 36 per cent depending on the sources of loan. The Utkal Gramya Bank and Central Cooperative Bank charged the minimum amount of interest of about 8 to 12 per cent per annum. The public sector banks also charge interest rate in between 8 to 15 per cent depending on the loan amount and time period. The farmers those who are landless and working on the rented, leased and community owned land or in case of *podu* cultivation where the cultivator has no rights over their land are not able to get any financial assistance from any institutional sources. These people are the worst sufferers. In the tribal society, majority of the people have no land records on their own and that is why they are deprived of many benefits provided by the government and other institutions. The literacy rate among the people of the study area is very low. The tribal and rural cultivators particularly are mostly illiterate and isolated. These people are not aware of the government schemes being implemented for their benefits. It is reported during the discussion with the people of some watershed villages that the bank people are not cooperative in providing individual or group loans (through SHGs).

It is reported that sometimes the farmers commit suicide by not being able to repay the loans. But in the backward Koraput region in general and in the sample watershed area in particular people die for not getting any financial help during their distress. Even the local moneylenders now-a-days do not provide loan without any mortgage. The indebtedness status of sample household during the pre- and post-watershed period is given in Table 5.19.

Table 5.19: Indebted Status of Sample Household in Pre- and Post-watershed Period

Sl.No.	*Type of Loan*	*Pre-watershed (No. of Households)*	*% of Total in Pre-watershed*	*Post-watershed (No. of Households)*	*% of Total in Post-watershed*
1.	Institutional	120	63.82	139	87.97
2.	Non-Institutional	68	36.18	19	12.03
3.	Production purpose	113	60.10	125	79.12
4.	Consumption purpose	75	39.90	33	20.88

Source: Household Survey 2008-09.

As it can be seen from Table 5.19 that the borrowing from Institutional sources has increased from about 64 per cent in pre-watershed period (2002-03) to about 88 per cent in post-watershed period (2006-07). This implies that the people after the watershed project period availed the loan from bank and other financial institutions more than they did before the watershed projects. One of the reasons for this trend may be the formation of Self-Help Groups (SHGs) in the watershed areas and their linkages with banks. It may be mentioned here that formation of SHGs is given priority in watershed villages.

Another positive trend found in this direction is that the loan for production purpose has increased in the post-watershed period than in the pre-w/s period. About 60 per cent of the loan was used for the production purpose in pre-watershed period which has increased to about 79 per cent in the post-watershed period. The increase in share of loan for productive purpose is a good sign for the repayment point of view. Out of the 300 households, 188 (62.6%) had taken credit during the pre-watershed period but in the year 2006-07 (Post-watershed) only 158 (52.6%) households had taken loan from all sources. The detailed watershed-wise indebtedness status of sample household is provided in Table 5.20. At the time of survey the total loan amount disbursed from all sources was ₹ 21,36,100. Out of this ₹ 5,92,700 (27.7%) has been repaid and ₹ 15,43,400 (72.3%) was outstanding.

Status of Water Table in Pre- and Post-watershed Period

An attempt was made to collect data on minimum and maximum level of groundwater for the year 2002-03 and 2006-07. In another column, the approximate rise/fall in water table in post-watershed period over the pre-watershed period is given. It is evident from the figures provided in Figures 5.15 and 5.16 that the water table for all the 14 blocks except Boipariguda has increased and for Jeypore block the minimum water table has fallen during the year 2006-07 as compared to the water level of 2002-03. Out of the 5 blocks taken for sample study only Boipariguda block has recorded a negative growth in water level in post-watershed period. The other 4 blocks, *viz.* Borigumma, Pottangi, Semiliguda, and Laxmipur have recorded an increase in the water table in the post-watershed period as compared to pre-watershed period. In Table 5.21, the water table of all the 14 blocks of Koraput district has been given.

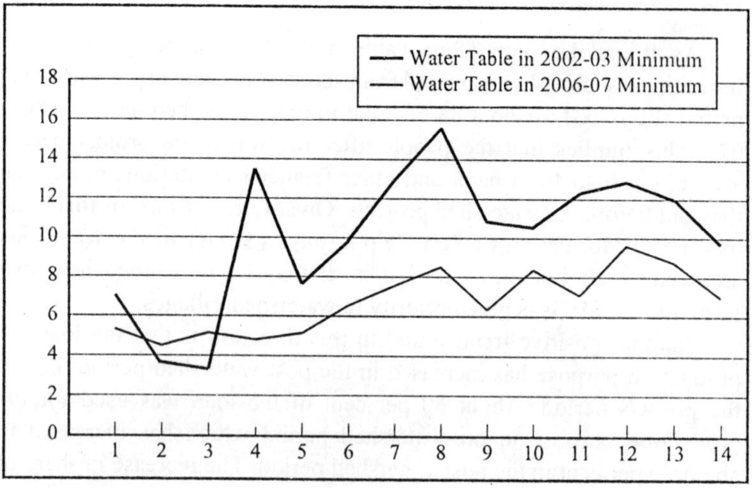

Source: RWSS, Koraput.

Figure 5.15: Change in Water Table (minimum) in Pre- and Post-watershed Period

Table 5.20: Indebtedness Status of Sample Households of Koraput District

Sl.No.	Name of Watershed	Source of Loan		Purpose of Loan		Loan Amount	Amount Repaid	Outstanding Loan
		Institutional	Non-Institutional	Production	Consumption			
1.	Panasput	13	1	9	5	1,72,000	22,000	1,50,000
2.	Kankadambo	3	0	2	1	25,000	—	25,000
3.	Ranikana	9	2	8	3	1,67,000	42,000	1,25,000
4.	Pomi	8	3	7	4	1,58,000	31,000	1,27,000
5.	Badaliguda	7	0	7	0	1,65,000	32,000	1,33,000
6.	Badapadu	8	0	7	1	92,600	29,000	63,600
7.	Girliguda	5	4	5	4	1,47,000	19,000	1,28,000
8.	Malkarbandh	5	0	5	0	1,16,000	72,000	44,000
9.	Jujhari	7	0	7	0	75,000	50,000	25,000
10.	Khandiguda	9	0	9	0	1,28,000	16,000	1,12,000
11.	Lodijodi	7	2	6	3	59,000	35,000	24,000
12.	Jodabandh	6	1	6	1	77,000	14,000	63,000
13.	Nandanmala	2	0	2	0	35,000	15,000	20,000
14.	Bodaguda	4	0	4	0	38,000	6,000	32,000
15.	Atalguda	2	0	1	1	4,000	—	4,000
16.	Majhiguda	7	1	6	2	37,000	12,000	25,000
17.	Marbaiguda	9	2	9	2	1,99,000	64,000	1,35,000
18.	Maligaon	10	0	9	1	1,34,000	28,500	1,05,500
19.	Bandikar	9	1	7	3	1,49,000	85,000	64,000
20.	Timajhola	9	2	9	2	1,58,500	20,200	1,38,300
	Total	**139**	**19**	**125**	**33**	**21,36,100**	**5,92,700**	**15,43,400**

Source: Household Survey, 2008-09.

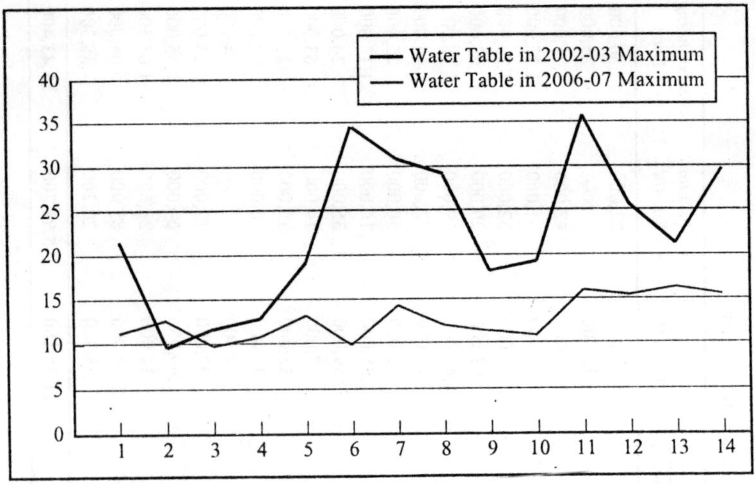

Source: RWSS, Koraput.

Figure 5.16: Change in Water Table (maximum) in Pre- and Post-watershed Period

Table 5.21: Status of Water Table in Various Blocks of Koraput District in 2002-03 and 2006-07

Sl.No.	*Name of the Block*	*Water Table in 2002-03*		*Water Table in 2006-07*		*Approx. Rise/Fall in Water Table*	
		Minimum	*Maximum*	*Minimum*	*Maximum*	*Minimum*	*Maximum*
1.	Borigumma	6.90	21.50	5.40	11.70	+1.50	+ 9.80
2.	Boipariguda	3.80	9.65	4.80	12.30	–1.00	– 2.65
3.	Jeypore	3.55	12.00	5.30	9.80	–1.75	+ 2.20
4.	Kundura	11.30	12.50	4.90	10.10	+6.40	+ 2.40
5.	Kotapd	7.85	18.90	5.30	13.20	+2.55	+ 5.70
6.	Koraput	9.75	34.33	6.30	9.90	+3.45	+24.43
7.	Lamtaput	12.85	31.00	7.40	14.00	+5.45	+17.00
8.	Nandapur	15.60	29.00	8.50	12.60	+7.10	+16.40
9.	Pottangi	10.80	17.80	6.30	12.10	+4.50	+ 5.70
10.	Semiliguda	10.70	18.25	8.30	11.40	+2.40	+ 6.85
11.	Bandhugaon	12.10	35.65	7.20	16.00	+4.90	+19.65
12.	Dasmantpur	12.70	25.93	9.50	15.30	+3.20	+10.63
13.	Laxmipur	12.00	22.00	8.70	16.40	+3.30	+ 5.60
14.	Narayanpatna	9.70	29.40	7.10	15.30	+2.60	+14.10

Source: Rural Water and Sanitation Works, Koraput 2010.

Availability of Safe Drinking Water

The availability of safe drinking water is very important for the general health and hygiene of the people. The rural people suffer from various diseases through the contaminated water from the pond, stream and other sources particularly during the rainy season. In the study area of the district the people depend on tubewell, spring based well, ponds, streams for their water requirements. It is alleged by the people during the survey that some of the tubewells are not functioning for a very long period of time in spite of several complaints by the local people to the block and district authorities. In many cases the surroundings of the tubewell is not properly cleaned and water is logging around the platform of the tubewells. Most of the people of the study area (as well as in the district) are not getting drinking water from safe sources like tubewells and spring based purified water supply system throughout the year. They have to drink water from ponds and streams nearer to the village which are mostly unhygienic. The availability of safe drinking water in pre- and post-watershed period of the 20 sample watersheds of the district is given in Figure 5.17. It is found from Figure 5.17 that during the period 2002-03, the average of availability of safe drinking water to all the watershed of the district was only 270 days and the same increased to 326 days in 2006-07. In the session 2002-03, there were only two watershed villages where people were getting supply of safe drinking water throughout the year which increased to eight watershed villages in

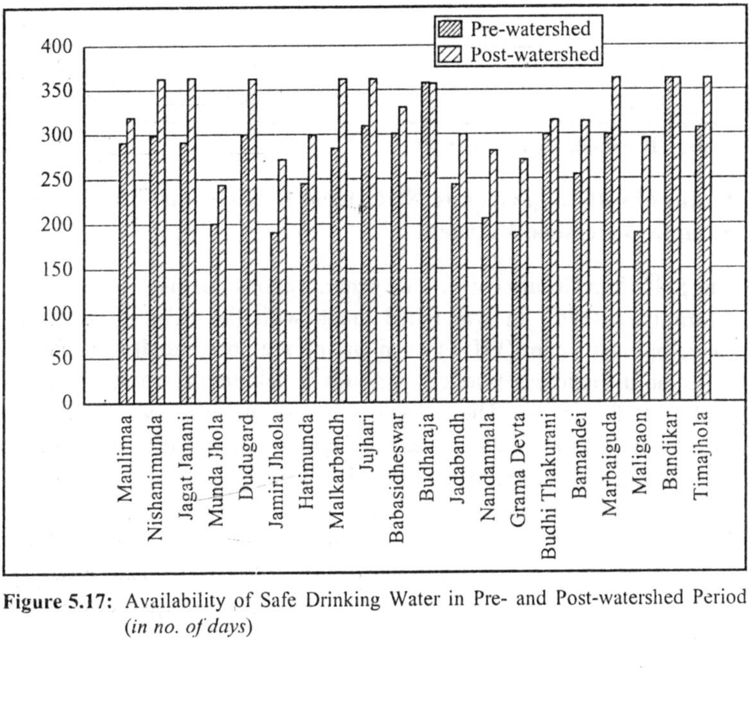

Figure 5.17: Availability of Safe Drinking Water in Pre- and Post-watershed Period *(in no. of days)*

the year 2006-07. The detailed data on the availability of safe drinking water in sample watershed area is given in Table 5.22.

Table 5.22: Availability of Safe Drinking Water in Pre- and Post-watershed (*in days*)

Sl.No.	*Name of Watershed*	*Block*	*Availability of Drinking Water in Days*	
			Pre-watershed	*Post-watershed*
1.	Panasput	Semiliguda	280	320
2.	Kankadambo	Semiliguda	300	365
3.	Ranikana	Semiliguda	280	365
4.	Pomi	Semiliguda	200	240
5.	Badaliguda	Pottangi	300	365
6.	Badapadu	Pottangi	180	270
7.	Girliguda	Pottangi	240	300
8.	Malkarbandh	Pottangi	270	365
9.	Jujhari	Borigumma	320	365
10.	Khandiguda	Borigumma	300	330
11.	Lodijodi	Borigumma	365	365
12.	Jodabandh	Borigumma	240	300
13.	Nandanmala	Boipariguda	210	280
14.	Bodaguda	Boipariguda	180	270
15.	Atalguda	Boipariguda	300	320
16.	Majhiguda	Boipariguda	260	320
17.	Marbaiguda	Laxmipur	300	365
18.	Maligaon	Laxmipur	180	290
19.	Bandikar	Laxmipur	365	365
20.	Timajhola	Laxmipur	320	365
	Total		**5,390**	**6,525**
	Average		**269.5**	**326.25**

Source: Household Survey, 2008-09.

Status of Self-Help Groups (SHGs) and User Groups (UGs) in the Sample Watershed Villages

The Self-Help Groups (SHGs) are generally constituted by the Watershed Committee (WC) in watershed areas with the help of Watershed Development Team (WDT) from among the poor, small and marginal households, landless/assetless agricultural labourers, women, shepherd and SC/ST persons. The emphasis has been given on formation of women SHGs in the study area. The number of women SHGs is about 90 per cent of the total SHGs formed in the study area and most of these SHGs belong to either ST or SC communities. In the sample watershed area, there are a total number of 211 SHGs. Out of this, 151 are Grade-I and 60 are of Grade-II level. As per the Swarna Jayanti Swarojagar Yojana (SGSY) guidelines, the SHGs which have completed at least six months of existence are treated as Grade-II SHGs and they are eligible for bank loan and subsidy. The total amount of savings by all these SHGs of the study area have been estimated to ₹ 20,18,179. Out of the total 211 numbers of SHGs 121 are bank linked and availing loans for economic activities like agriculture, mushroom cultivation, pisciculture, *dal* processing, sugarcane processing and other activities like small trades and business.

The members of the SHG groups regularly contribute to the common fund of the Group according to their capacity. In most of the cases it is found that there are 10 members from one homogenous group and contribute ₹ 5 or ₹ 10 per week to the common fund. In some places the members are contributing even more than the minimum prescribed amount per week but all the members of one individual group usually contribute the same amount. The members of the groups which have attained the Grade-II status and have started some economic activities approach the banks for financial assistance under the SGSY scheme. The SHG movement in the district has contributed towards the economic and social empowerment of the ST/SC and underprivileged women.

The user groups are those persons who have landholdings within the watershed area and are deriving direct benefit from a particular watershed scheme or activity. In the sample watershed area there are 611 numbers of user groups. They have contributed ₹ 27,35,921 towards the Watershed Development Fund (WDF). The Jodabandh watershed of Borigumma block has the maximum number of user groups (52) with a contribution of ₹ 1,86,497 to WDF. The watershed-wise detail figure for the SHGs and UGs are given in Table 5.24. The WDT fund is being utilized by the watershed committee of the concerned watersheds for the repair and maintenance of the projects only after the completion of the project period (Table 5.23).

Table 5.23: Scheme-wise Status of SHGs/UGs of the District

Sl.No.	*Scheme*	*No. of Watershed*	*No. of SHGs*	*Savings (₹ in lakh)*	*No. of User Groups*	*WDF (₹ in lakh)*
1.	EAS	72	566	71.23	2,172	62.98
2.	ACA	84	930	128.49	2,937	185.00
3.	IWDP-IV	24	248	23.87	919	24.75
4.	IWDP-V	10	85	12.09	274	19.28
5.	IWDP-VI	10	40	3.21	96	3.84
6.	IWDP-VII	10	48	8.90	37	3.00
	Total	**210**	**1,917**	**247.79**	**6,435**	**298.85**

SHG — Self-Help Group, WDF — Watershed Development Fund.
Source: DRDA, Koraput, 2010.

Table 5.24: Status of SHGs/UGs Formed in Sample Watershed Projects

Sl.No.	*Block*	*Scheme*	*Name of W/S*	*Level of SHGs*		*Amount Saved*	*Bank Linkages*	*No. of UG Formed*	*Amount of WDF*
				Grade-I	*Grade-II*				
1.	Semiliguda	ACA	Panasput	9	2	1,08,000	7	22	1,10,000
2.	Semiliguda	ACA	Kankadambo	10	3	1,12,250	6	29	1,10,000
3.	Semiliguda	ACA	Ranikana	8	3	1,06,000	6	31	1,10,000
4.	Semiliguda	ACA	Pomi	7	5	92,650	8	27	1,05,000
5.	Pottangi	ACA	Badaliguda	11	3	60,000	3	29	1,38,315
6.	Pottangi	ACA	Badapadu	13	4	78,500	6	27	1,20,500
7.	Pottangi	ACA	Girliguda	9	3	60,000	12	25	1,88,000
8.	Pottangi	EAS	Malkarbandh	3	0	79,000	3	30	47,771
9.	Borigumma	ACA	Jujhari	6	2	1,22,000	6	24	1,35,600
10.	Borigumma	ACA	Khandiguda	7	3	1,39,000	7	22	1,24,200
11.	Borigumma	ACA	Lodijodi	6	3	84,779	5	29	2,21,718
12.	Borigumma	ACA	Jodabandh	4	1	99,600	5	52	1,86,497
13.	Boipariguda	ACA	Nandanmala	5	4	1,13,300	4	32	1,28,350
14.	Boipariguda	ACA	Bodaguda	6	3	1,18,100	5	30	1,22,670
15.	Boipariguda	ACA	Atalguda	7	4	1,22,000	5	31	1,24,700
16.	Boipariguda	ACA	Majhiguda	7	2	1,09,800	5	29	1,29,100
17.	Laxmipur	ACA	Marbaiguda	9	3	1,03,400	6	36	1,73,000
18.	Laxmipur	ACA	Maligaon	8	5	1,05,000	7	33	1,69,300
19.	Laxmipur	ACA	Bandikar	8	4	1,06,200	7	34	1,80,500
20.	Laxmipur	EAS	Timajhola	8	3	98,600	8	39	1,10,700
	Total			**151**	**60**	**20,18,179**	**121**	**611**	**27,35,921**

Source: District Rural Development Agency, Koraput, 2010.

Perception of the Community on Watershed Development Programmes

One of the objectives of this study is to assess the impact of watershed programme as perceived by the community. The participation of community in the watershed programme is the basic philosophy behind the formation of watershed. In this section, the perception of the people of the sample household on watershed development programme is discussed. The views of the beneficiaries about the impact of the watershed development programmes on various bio-physical and socio-economic aspects are given in Table 5.25. It is perceived by the majority of the households that the soil and moisture conservation has been the major positive impact of the watershed programme which has resulted in better yield of various crops. The increase in the groundwater level is the effect of water harvesting on watershed basis. People's perception is that there is an increase in the availability of drinking water for human consumption as well as for the livestock. It is also revealed by the beneficiaries that the land value has considerably increased on account of its increased fertility and productivity. The employment potential in the locality has also increased after the watershed projects being implemented.

Table 5.25: Perception on Impact of WDPs by the Members of the Sample Households

Sl.No.	*Variable*	*Percentage of Households*
1.	Soil conservation	71
2.	Moisture conservation	64
3.	Better Yield	59
4.	Fodder and fuel availability	26
5.	Increase in groundwater table	35
6.	Increase in drinking water availability in no. of days	36
7.	Employment generation	42
8.	Increase in land value	27
9.	Checking migration	32

Source: Household Survey, 2008-09.

Most of the sample households feel that the water harvesting structures constructed in the watersheds have directly helped to increase the moisture conservation in the soil and have to raise the groundwater level. The importance of various soil conservation measures like nala bund, diversion weir, check dam, gully control and farm pond are already known to the beneficiaries of these projects. It is perceived by the people of the area that these structures restricted the flow of groundwater run-off and improved the *in-situ* moisture conservation. The farmers of the watershed area are aware of the importance of these structures in rainfed farming system. In Table 5.26, the percentage opinion of sample households who perceive an increase in moisture conservation and increase in groundwater table due to different water arresting structures has been given. The nala bund (46%) and check dam (52%) are the main structures which arrest the soil erosion and increase moisture conservation as it has been revealed by the people of the sample watersheds.

Table 5.26: Perception on Increase in Moisture Conservation and Groundwater Level

Sl.No.	*Structures*	*Percentage of Household*
1.	Nala Bund	46
2.	Check Dam	52
3.	Farm Ponds	35
4.	Gully Checks	24
5.	Vegetative Bunds	31
6.	No Idea	11

Source: Household Survey, 2008-09.

The sample household's response to the construction of various structures for the control of soil erosion is presented in Table 5.27. Bunds of different kinds have predominantly dominated in arresting the soil erosion in the sample watershed area. The other soil conservation activities like the block plantation, gully checks, diversion channel are comparatively less significant in checking the erosion as perceived by the community, but their importance depend on landscape and geographical condition which have also helped to some extent in controlling soil erosion.

Table 5.27: Perception on Checking Soil Erosion Through Different Activities

Sl.No.	*Structures*	*Percentage of Household*
1.	Bunds	22
2.	Vegetative bunds/small bunds	43
3.	Block Plantation	54
4.	Gully Checks	48
5.	No Idea	14

Source: Household Survey, 2008-09.

Under the convergence scheme the various government departments are functioning for the development of the watershed areas in an integrated manner. One of the activities is that of the plantation by the forest and soil conservation department in the watershed villages. The impact of block plantation on the life of the people of the area and on the ecology of the area as perceived by the community is presented in Table 5.28. It is reported by the respondents that the main impact of block plantation is that of eased out fuel problem, increase in rainy days and reduction in fodder problems for the livestock apart from others. The percentage of people feel that the impacts of plantation on the various benefits they receive are given in Table 5.28.

Table 5.28: Perception on Impact of Block Plantation

Sl.No.	*Perceptions*	*Percentage of Household*
1.	Labour employment	42
2.	Eased out fuel problems	32
3.	Increase in rainy days	18
4.	Increase in fodder availability	39
5.	Controlling soil erosion	13
6.	Availability of green manure	6
7.	No idea	12

Source: Household Survey, 2008-09.

It is found from Table 5.28 that 39 per cent of the total sample households feel that there has been increase in fodder availability due to the plantations and 32 per cent feel that it has reduced firewood problem and 18 per cent of them feel that there has been an increase in the number of rainy days due to block plantation.

The involvement of the community in the watershed development programmes is one of the important criteria for the success of the WDPs. The perception of the community on involvement in various stages of watershed programme is presented in Table 5.29. From the household survey, it is clear that the people of the watershed area are interested in involving themselves in the various stages of the WDPs.

Table 5.29: Sample Households Perception as Regard to Involvement in WDPs

Sl.No.	*Involvement is Necessary*	*Percentage of Household*
1.	Yes	68
2.	No	21
3.	No Idea	11

Source: Household Survey, 2008-09.

Regarding the participation in WDPs, 68 per cent of the total household feel that it is essential on their part to involve themselves in various stages of WDPs and 21 per cent feel it is not necessary for them and 11 per cent have no idea about the same. It is also reported that out of 300 households, 62 per cent regularly attend the meetings organized in the village.

The community people who reported their involvement is necessary in WDPs were further questioned as to at which stage of implementation they feel it is necessary to be involved. The opinion expressed by the sample household is that they want to be involved in all stages of implementation. The opinion of the people regarding their involvement is presented in Table 5.30. In all the three stages of implementation, i.e. planning, implementation and maintenance, the local community is interested in participation.

Table 5.30: Participation of the Communities in the WDPs

Sl.No.	*Stages of Implementation*	*Percentage of Household*
1.	Planning	38
2.	Implementation	43
3.	Maintenance	34
4.	Not Interested	18

Source: Household Survey, 2008-09.

The suggestions for improving the watershed development projects as perceived by the community are presented in Table 5.31. The suggestion that were pointed out are more water harvesting structures like nala bund, check dams and farm pond for the better utilization of run-off water and it can be utilized for the use of livestock and for irrigating horticultural crops during the dry period. The other suggestions include the easy availability of agricultural loan, remunerative price and marketing facility for the farm products, etc.

Table 5.31: Sample Households Perception Regarding Improvement of WDPs

Sl.No.	*Suggestions*	*Percentage of Household*
1.	Water harvesting structures	42
2.	Participation of the community	32
3.	Agricultural loan/Marketing facility	36
4.	Cash crops	18
5.	Post project period maintenance	20
6.	No idea	12

Source: Household Survey, 2008-09.

The sample households feel that the socio-economic status of the people through WDPS can be improved by creating more water harvesting structures, more involvement of people in the process, availability of farm loan, marketing facility for the agricultural products, post-project period maintenance and from cereal to cash crops.

Summary

The success or failure of any project is judged from its performance in fulfilling the objectives laid down in the project. The successful implementation of the programme in watershed development programme is expected to bring the twin benefits of soil and water conservation and enhancing the livelihoods of the rural poor. Some of the broad-based development objectives under the projects are increasing the irrigation potential of the watershed area and hence the agricultural productivity of the area, restoring ecological balance in the degraded and fragile ecosystem, reducing regional disparity between irrigated and non-irrigated areas and creation of sustained employment opportunity for the rural poor.

In the watershed area, there has been an increase in irrigation potential in the post-watershed period as compared to the pre-watershed period. In the post-watershed period the irrigated area rose to about 47 per cent of the total sample watershed area as compared to 31 per cent in pre-watershed period (Tables 5.7 and 5.8). The wasteland has been reduced from 36.25 acres in pre-watershed period to 14.50 acres in post-watershed period. In the sample watershed area, the productivity of major agricultural commodities too has increased in post-watershed period as compared to pre-watershed period. More or less all the major agricultural commodities have registered a positive growth in the post-watershed period (Table 5.9 and Figure 5.6). It is also observed that in the post-watershed period there has been crop diversification from paddy to non-paddy crops. The cropping intensity of the sample area has also increased from 122 per cent in pre-watershed period to 176 per cent in post-watershed period.

After the implementation of the WDPs, the water table of the area has increased to a marked extent (Table 5.21). The availability of safe drinking water has also improved in the post-project period.

During the post-watershed period there has been an increase in the share of income of agriculture in the total income of the sample household. The percentage share of agriculture which was 18.22 per cent in pre-watershed period increased to 22.99 per cent in post-watershed period (Figure 5.12). In the post-watershed period, the population of livestock and the income from livestock has increased in the post-watershed period in comparison to pre-watershed period. The share of livestock income in the total income of the households has increased from 10.39 per cent in pre-w/s period to 12.27 per cent in post-w/s period (Tables 5.11 and 5.12). The growth in the livestock population and productivity of the animals has increased in the post-project period on account of the better availability of fodder and drinking water for them in this period. In the post-project period the share of income from labour has increased in absolute value though the percentage share of labour income in the total income has reduced as compared to the pre-project period. It is observed by the scholar that in the study area during the project period and after its completion the scope of earning through wage employment has increased. This has resulted in the reduction in the migration from villages after the watershed project started in these areas.

Food security of the sample household has also improved in post-project period as compared to the pre-project period. In the post-watershed period 27.66 per cent of the total household were food secured for 12 months as compared to 9.33 per cent in pre-watershed period (Table 5.15). The per capita income and expenditure in the post-project period has also increased as compared to pre-watershed period. It has been observed that 50 per cent of the sample watersheds have crossed the BPL line in the post-project period based on the expenditure criteria fixed by Tendulkar Committee for the rural people of Odisha. In the pre-project period all the 20 watersheds were coming under the BPL category as per the Tendulkar Committee's expenditure criteria (Table 5.14). It implies that the sample household are leading a better life than before.

In the sample watershed area, the total savings of sample watershed increased from ₹ 3,36,900 in pre-watershed period to ₹ 22,85,800 in post-watershed period. The importance of banks in mobilizing the savings has increased during this period. In the sample analysis it was found that in the post-watershed period the role of institutional sources of finance has increased in providing loans to 87.97 per cent borrowing households as compared to 63.82 per cent in pre-watershed period. Similarly, the loan for production purpose has increased from 60 per cent to 79 per cent in the post-watershed period. It is clear that the banking habit of the sample households has increased in the post-watershed period.

The formation of Self-Help Groups in the watershed areas has particularly empowered the women of the area. The participation of the community in various capacity-building programmes has also helped them becoming self-sufficient.

6

SUMMARY AND CONCLUSIONS

Conclusions

On the basis of the study conducted in five blocks of Koraput district with 300 households as the sample size, some broad conclusions have emerged with regards to the impact of the watershed development programmes on the stakeholders of the area. This chapter attempts to present the conclusions emerged from the entire study. The various hypotheses taken for the study have been verified in this chapter and at the end of the chapter some humble suggestions have been made for improving the performance of the project.

The watershed approach of development is a paradigm shift from the earlier plot based approach to soil and water conservation. This approach intends to harmonize the use of soil, water and vegetation in a way that conserves these resources and maximize their productivity. The main objective of a watershed development project is to achieve sustainable production of biomass and restoration of ecological balance in drought prone and rainfed areas, thereby improving people's standard of living.

The concept of sustainable livelihood was emerged during 1990s. This grew from the awareness that rural development approach based purely on agricultural production were insufficient to meet livelihood needs of the rural and landless poor. It must be remembered that the key to any watershed project and its sustainability depends on the community participation at the various stages of the project implementation.

The study was mainly undertaken to know the extent of irrigation potential created, productivity of land increased, crop diversification taken place, ecological balance maintained and overall socio-economic development of the people achieved under watershed programme in sample blocks of Koraput district. It may be noted that majority of the beneficiaries here are the tribals.

It is found from the sample study that irrigation, which is the most important factor in increasing the crop productivity, has increased in the post-watershed period as compared to the pre-watershed period (see Table 5.7 and Figure 5.6). The percentage share of irrigated land to the total land of the sample study area has increased in the post-watershed period. Similarly, the quantity of wasteland has declined in the post-watershed period. It is observed from the sample study that due to the implementation of the watershed projects in these areas there has been a substantial increase in the irrigation potential of the areas in post-project period as compared to the pre-project period. In the post-watershed period, the total irrigated area of the study area increased to 47 per cent of the total land area from 31 per cent in the pre-watershed period. The farmers of the sample area are now utilizing their land more for the multiple cropping than they did it before. The cropping intensity of the sample study area has also registered a positive growth in the post-watershed project. The cropping intensity which was 126 per cent in the pre-watershed period has increased to 176 per cent in the post-watershed period.

The findings of the study show that the overall irrigation potential of the sample watershed area and the cropping intensity of the area has increased during the post-watershed period. In the post-project period more and more wasteland are now brought into the fold of cultivable land.

Agriculture which is the main occupation of 85 per cent of the sample households in the study area has registered a higher yield rate in the post-watershed period than the pre-watershed period. For example, all 20 crops taken for the sample study have registered a positive growth. The per hectare yield has increased from 4 per cent in niger to 240 per cent in cabbage.

Implementation of watershed programme has contributed to growth of animal population in the study area. In the sample study it was found that during the post-watershed period the population of Cattle, Buffalo, Goat, Sheep, Poultry and Pigs have increased substantially as compared to the pre-watershed period (see Table 5.10) The share of income from livestock in the total household income has increased during the post-watershed period as compared to the pre-watershed period. The share of income from livestock in the total income of the household has increased from 10.39 per cent in pre-watershed period to 12.27 per cent in post-watershed period. It can be well inferred that on account of better availability of fodder in the sample watershed area, the livestock population as well as the income from livestock has increased in course of time.

It is found from the study that the share of income from sale of non-timber forest products (NTFP) in the total income of the sample household has shown a declining trend in the post-watershed period in comparison to pre-watershed period. It is interesting to note that in spite of the fact that the forest cover and block plantation of the sample has increased over the years, the share of income from NTFP in total income of the household in the post-project period has come down. Out of the 20 sample watersheds in the sample, in the case of 16 watersheds, the income from NTFP in post-watershed period has declined in comparison to that of the pre-watershed period. One of the reasons of this trend might be that the people of the watershed area got alternative works which were more remunerative than the collection and sale of NTFP. At the same time whatever NTFPs they collected were mostly used for domestic consumption. The village people of watershed area are now engaged in agricultural activities for a longer period of time than before due to the increase in irrigation facility. At the same time, they are now getting wage employment opportunity in various employment guarantee schemes and other such activities.

We may summarize the findings in the following lines. There has been an increase in agricultural productivity in sample watershed area due to the availability of better irrigation facility. The livestock population and income from livestock has also increased due to the increased fodder availability and sufficient availability of drinking water for the livestock. The income from other sources like small business, service and other miscellaneous works has also increased during this period.

It is important to mention here that even though the share of labour in the total income of the sample households in post-watershed period has declined, it is still the single largest contributor to the income of the sample households in the post-watershed period.

Implementation of watershed programme has contributed to the extent and pattern of expenditure of the beneficiaries. In the post-watershed period, the sample household's share of expenditure on food items has decreased from 52 per cent in pre-watershed period to 43 per cent in post-watershed period though food still remains as the single largest item of expenditure in the budget of the sample households. The expenditure of sample household in post-project period on clothing, housing, education, health, fuel and festivals, etc. have increased in comparison to the pre-watershed period. A rise in the income level shows a shift of expenditure from food items to non-food items.

The per capita expenditure per month of all the twenty sample watersheds have registered a positive growth in the post-watershed period. As per the report of Expert Group on Estimation of Poverty (Tendulkar Committee, 2009) by the Planning Commission, Government of India, the minimum expenditure of ₹ 407.78 for the rural population of Odisha was taken as the poverty line. The base year of calculation of poverty line was 2004. If we compare the level of per capita expenditure of our sample population with the estimation of the Expert Group then all the sample households in the watershed areas on an average lived below the poverty line during the pre-watershed period. However, in the post-watershed period, the per capita per month expenditure of 10 watersheds out of the total 20 watersheds taken as sample, showed that the people have remained above the poverty line (based on Tendulkar Committee estimates). It may be mentioned here that the above figures projected with reference to expert group estimation on poverty taking 2004-05 as the base year, without making any adjustments taking into account the rate of inflation during these periods. This comparison has been made without making any adjustment due to inflation between the base year of 2004-05 of the Expert Group and our study period between 2002-03 and 2006-07. But one thing becomes clear that there has been a positive change in the standard of living of the people living in sample watershed area, as a result of which on an average 50 per cent of them have crossed the poverty line in the post-watershed period.

As far as the issue of food security of the sample households is concerned, there has been an improvement in the food security in the post-project period as compared to the pre-project period. In the post-watershed period about 28 per cent of the total households were food secured for the whole year which was only 9 per cent in the pre-watershed period (Table 5.15 and Figure 5.13). It may be inferred that on account of the implementation of the watershed projects in the sample watershed area there has been an improvement in the foodgrain production and also the level of income which in turn has improved the food security position of the sample households in the post-project period than that of the pre-project period.

One of the important findings of the study is that the gross savings of the sample households has considerably increased in the post-watershed period as compared to the pre-watershed period. The banking habit of the sample household has also improved in the post-watershed period as people prefer to save their money with the banks rather than keeping it at home or with the post office. People now borrow money more from the institutional sources like the banks and other financial institutions. The importance of non-institutional sources of borrowing has declined during this period. It is pertinent to mention here that the institutions like the watershed committee and the self-help groups play an important role in linking their financial requirements to the banks. Another important finding of the study is that in the post-watershed period the borrowed funds are mostly used for the productive purposes rather than for consumption purposes (See Table 5.19).

An attempt has been made to collect data on minimum and maximum level of groundwater for the year 2002-03 and 2006-07. The data collected from the secondary sources reveal that in most part of the district the water table in the minimum and maximum level has increased substantially in the year post-project period (2006-07) in comparison to pre-project period (2002-03). Out of the five blocks taken as sample only one block, i.e. Boipariguda has recorded a negative growth in the post-watershed period. The other four blocks, *viz.* Borigumma, Pottangi, Semiliguda and Laxmipur have recorded an increase in the water table in the post-watershed period as compared to the pre-watershed period (see Table 5.21 and Figures 5.15 and 5.16).

Another positive contribution of the implementation of watershed project is that in the sample watershed villages, the availability of safe drinking water has improved. The data collected from the sample households reveals that in the sample watershed villages the availability of safe drinking water has increased in most of the watershed areas. In the pre-watershed period, the availability of safe drinking water for the entire watershed area was 270 days which has increased to 326 days in the post-watershed period. In the pre-project period there were only two watersheds which were getting safe drinking water throughout the year but in the post-project period the same has gone up to eight.

Another important aspect to be noticed is that the area under tree cover has increased substantially in the post-watershed period due to the block plantation by soil conservation, forest and horticulture departments. The number of water bodies in and around the watershed villages has also increased. The people of the area agreed that the soil, moisture and bio-mass conservation of the sample watershed area has improved in the post-watershed period than that of the pre-project period.

With the initiative taken and incentives provided in the watershed area, there have been formation of a large number of User Groups (UGs) and Self-Help Groups (SHGs). Some of the SHG groups are undertaking various economic activities like mushroom cultivation, *dal* processing, agricultural activities, pisciculture, sugarcane processing, small business, etc. It is important to mention here that in the tribal dominated district of Koraput about 90 per cent of the total SHGs are operated by the women. It is noteworthy to mention here that the SHG movement in the watershed area of the district has not only empowered the women of the area economically but also politically.

The beneficiaries of the sample blocks have admitted that on account of the implementation of the watershed programmes there has been an improvement in the field of employment generation and the value of their land has also gone up on account of an increase in irrigation facility. The community members admitted that the watershed programme has been successful in checking migration to a great extent.

The community members further opined that the water harvesting structures like nala bund, check dam, farm ponds, gully checks had helped in conserving the moisture and improving the water table of the area. Similarly, the bunds, block plantation, gully checks have contributed towards checking soil erosion to a great extent and also improved the soil health in the watershed areas.

The massive plantation programme undertaken by the forest and soil conservation department through the convergence scheme has benefitted the sample villagers in many aspects. Among other benefits reaped by the villagers the above activity has created labour employment opportunity for the villagers, eased out their fuel problems and increased availability of fodder for the livestock population.

Verification of Hypotheses

As it has been revealed through the sample study, there has been an increase in the irrigation potential in the post-watershed period which in turn has increased the production of the various crops. On account of availability of irrigation facility the land could be better utilized in the sample watershed villages. Hence, the intensity of the land usage has increased in the post-watershed project period. This verifies the *first hypothesis* taken for the study that the watershed development programmes increase irrigation potential of the area.

Another welcome contribution of watershed programme in the study area is that almost every crop has registered a positive growth in the post-project period. It is also observed that there has been crop diversification from paddy to non-paddy crops, more importantly a majority of the farmers of the area are cultivating their field more than once. Some of the cash crops are now being produced by the cultivators of the area which were not produced earlier due to the lack of irrigation facility. All these confirm to the *second hypothesis* of the study that the agricultural productivity of various crops of the region has gone up significantly on account of the implementation of the watershed projects.

The water table in watershed area has increased. Among other things this has resulted in the better availability of the drinking water in the study villages. It has been earlier mentioned that the number of trees in the villages has substantially increased in the post-project period due to the block plantation by the soil conservation and forest departments. The increase in numbers of fruit bearing and firewood plants in the watershed area has not only supported the villagers economically but also it has improved the ecological condition of the entire area. The biomass and *in-situ* moisture conservation of the locality has improved which has resulted in the higher crop productivity. At the same time, the intensity of cropping has also improved in the study area. All these conform to the *third hypothesis* that the ecological condition of the area has improved due to the availability of water in the region.

The population of all the livestock in the watershed area has increased and the income from the livestock has also shown a positive trend. The availability of fodder and drinking water for livestock in the watershed area has also considerably increased which has supported the livestock population of the locality. The *fourth hypothesis* which assumes that the watershed projects have contributed towards the growth of livestock both in terms of quantity and quality is found to be true from the findings of this study.

It has been revealed from the sample study that there has been substantial growth in the income and expenditure levels of the sample households in the post-watershed period. The standard of living of the people has also improved considerably which can be found from the fact that in the year 2006-07, 50 per cent of the sample watershed villages have crossed the poverty line based on the expenditure criteria fixed by Tendulkar Committee taking 2004 as the base year. It is pertinent to mention here that in the pre-watershed period all the households in 20 watersheds had the income as well as the expenditure level which were below the poverty line. The saving status of the sample household has also improved during this period. In the post-project period, it has been found that the savings by the villagers has increased manyfolds as compared to the pre-project period. This has contributed towards the economic as well as socio-political empowerment of the beneficiaries of the watershed area. The women SHGs in the villages have not only improved their economic status but also got the strength to fight for their rights as a group against all types of exploitations which was denied to them earlier. All these confirm to the *fifth hypothesis* that the social and economic condition of the stakeholders of the watershed programmes has improved considerably.

Suggestions

Here follows a few humble suggestions to make the watershed programme perform better in a backward and tribal dominated locality like Koraput district:

- It is felt that the poor and landless farmers are not getting much of the benefits of the watershed projects. The externalities in the watershed programmes should be so managed that the gap between the small and big farmers should be minimized. More attention should be given to the poor and landless to enable them to have access to resources they need.
- In order to make the participatory approach of development more meaningful, the role of Non-Governmental Organizations (NGOs) is felt very important. The social organization part may be entrusted to the NGOs so that villagers can participate at different stages of project implementation.
- It is felt that more emphasis should be given on the withdrawal strategy of these projects so that the benefits of the projects can continue even after completion of the project period.
- Watershed Development Team members should be engaged prior to the implementation of the project to ensure proper implementation and their belongingness to the project.
- The Watershed Development Fund (WDF) should be kept in the form of fixed/term deposits from the first year onwards till the completion of the project so as to earn better rates of interest on the deposits.
- The local institutions and indigenous technologies of the tribal people of the area should be given respect while planning the development of that community.
- As far as possible various works may be entrusted to the SHGs rather than to other external agencies.
- More emphasis should be given in the projects for development of social aspects like the education and health of the villagers

particularly in the tribal areas like that of Koraput district. The economic development without social development is meaningless to achieve the goal of overall development.

- Further, measures may be initiated for the increase in income of the beneficiaries through horticulture, livestock and pisciculture which is not yet fully exploited.
- It is felt that the banks should cooperate more with the SHG groups and farmers in providing loans for productive purposes.
- The marketing facility for the agricultural products in terms of process and storage facilities may be strengthened for the farmers so that they are not exploited by the unscrupulous traders.
- The project period of a watershed development project should be at least 10 years and people should feel that the project is for their own benefits. The villagers are to be convinced that the facilities extended by the watershed and capacity-building programmes are meant to make them stand on their own leg in the years to come.
- All departmental programmes implemented in the district should be mandatorily converged in the watershed area to saturate the development process.
- The perspective planning for watershed programme should be made through a reputed/expert agency having experience in the field keeping in mind the local requirements.

PHOTOGRAPHS

Photo 1: Typical Kondha Village of Timajhola

Photo 2: Harvesting Time for the Farmers

Photo 3: Scholar Interacting with Konkodambo Villagers

Photo 4: The Villagers Using the Tubewell for Drinking Water

Photo 5: Indira Awas Houses under Convergence Scheme

Photo 6: Field Channel of a Watershed Project

Photo 7: PRA Exercise under Progress in Malkarbandh Village

Photo 8: Meeting Place of the Erasantaguda Village

Photo 9: Cashew Plantation under the Convergence Scheme

Photo 10: Women Cultivators Using the KB Pump for Irrigation

Photo 11: Spring Based Drinking Water in Pottangi Block

Photo 12: A Dug Well Used for Irrigation Purpose in Borigumma

Photo 13: Ginger Cultivation in Pottaugi Block

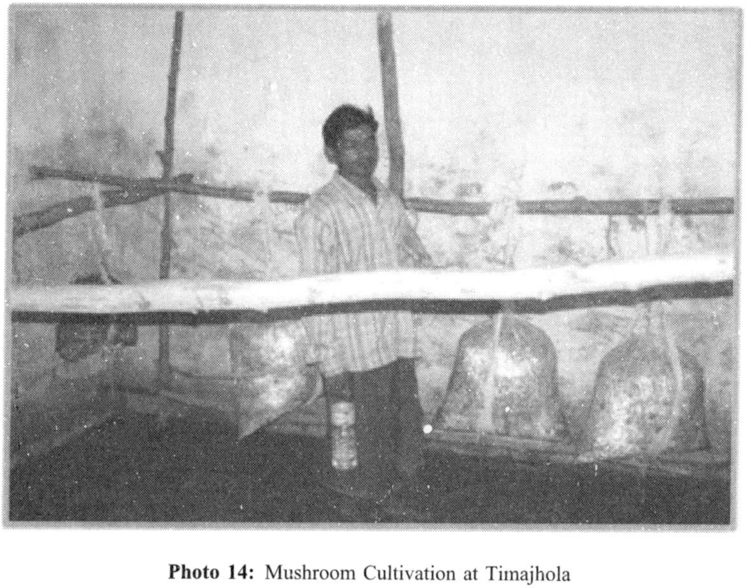

Photo 14: Mushroom Cultivation at Timajhola

Photo 15: Yam Cultivation in Semiliguda Block

Photo 16: A Greenhouse Developing Nursery at Boipariguda Block

Photo 17: Vermicompost Pit Prepared by the Farmers

Photo 18: Paddy Field in Borigumma Block

Photo 19: The Rearing of Banaraj Variety of Poultry

Photo 20: Livestock in Konkodambo Village

Photo 21: Papaya Farm Produced by the Farmers at Ranikona Village

Photo 22: Banana Crop on Tank Bund in Semiliguda Block

Photo 23: The Scholar Discussing with the Beneficiaries

Photo 24: Banana Cultivation in Semiliguda Block

ANNEXURES

Questionnaire for Household Survey

Name of the Block : ____________ Name of the Watershed : ________

Name of the Beneficiary : ____________________________

Category–ST/SC/Gen/Others : ____________ Name of the Sub Caste : ________

Name of the Village : ____________________________

Name of the G.P. : ____________________________

Starting year of the watershed: ____________________________

Date of survey : ____________________________

Household ID# : ____________________________

	2002-03	*2006-07*
Total Family Size		
Total Male adult		
Total Female adult		
Total Male child		
Total Female child		

General Observation of the Household (2006-07)

Sl.No.	*Name*	*Age*	*Sex*	*Marital Status*	*Education*	*Occupation*	
						Main	*Subsidiary*

Education
1st to 5th — 1
5th to 10th — 2
Above 10th — 3
Any other degree — 4
Balwadi/Anganwadi — 5
No education — 0

Sex
Male — M
Female — F
Male Child — MC
Female Child — FC

Marital Status
Married — M
Unmarried — UM

Occupation
Agriculture — 1
Labour — 2
Service — 3
Other (Specify) — 4

01	*2002-03*		*2006-07*	
Does this family belong to BPL Category? Yes — 1, No — 2				

Section – A

Income	*2002-03*	*2006-07*
1. What are the different sources of income of your family? ◆ Agriculture ◆ Labour ◆ Service ◆ Other (Specify)		
2. How many persons in your family are/were engaged in income generation activity?		
3. How many persons in your family are working as migrant labour?		
4. What is/was the aggregate income of your family per month?		
5. Is there any change in income of your family from 2002-03 to 2006-07? (For Yes — 1 and for No — 2) (if yes then ask how and why?)		

Section – B

Land Use and Agriculture Production	*2002-03*		*2006-07*	
1. How much land do you have? (in acres)				
2. How much of them are irrigated?				
3. How much of them are non-irrigated?				
4. How much of them are wasteland?				
5. How much of the wasteland are developed now?				
6. Do you use the same land more than a year? If yes, Area and no. of times.				
7. What do you produce in those lands?	*2002-03*		*2006-07*	
	Quantity	*Value*	*Quantity*	*Value*
# Monsoon # Winter # Summer				

8. Do/Did you cultivate Vegetables in those lands? (Yes — 1, No — 2)				
9. What are/were the vegetables you cultivate in your land? A. .... B. .... C. .... D. .... E.				
10. Availability of foodgrains out of the above production in months —				
11. Did you buy any more land? If yes then when?				
12. Did you sell any of your land?				
13. What is the value of your land?				

14. Tell me the changes you think in the quality of land after the intervention of watershed programme?		
15. Did you change your cropping pattern? If Yes, Specify		
16. Do you perform mixed cultivation in your land?		
17. What is the cost of cultivation (₹) per acre?		

Section – C

Livestock	*2002-03*		*2006-07*	
1. Do your family have livestock? (Yes — 1, No — 2)				
2. What are the livestock your family has? A. .... B. .... C. .... D. .... E.				
3. Do you sale them in the market? (if yes then calculate the selling price)				
4. What are the products you get from the livestock you have? A. .... B. .... C. .... D.	*Qty.*	*Value*	*Qty.*	*Value*

5. What do you use as fodder for your livestock and how much in a month? A. .... B. .... C.				
6. Do you get those fodders from the market, (if yes then what is the market rate)?	*Qty.*	*Value*	*Qty.*	*Value*
7. If no how much you collect or cultivate fodder in a month?				
8. Did you feel any change in livestock in these few years?				
9. If yes then tell me how?				

Section – D

Forestry and Water	*2002-03*	*2006-07*
1. Do you have Plantation in your own land? (Yes — 1, No — 2)		
2. If Yes, How much acre of land?		
3. Is there any forest in your village? (Yes — 1, No — 2)		
4. Do you go to nearby forest to collect NTFP?		
5. What are the NTFP you collect from the forest? A. .... B. .... C. .... D. .... E.		
6. Do you sell them in the market?		
7. What is the Market value of those products?		
8. Do you have your own pond/well?		
9. Do you get enough drinking water throughout the year and from where? (Yes — 1, No — 2) ◆ .... ◆ .... ◆		
10. If no, for how many days/months you do not get drinking water?		
11. Do you have your own pond or well?		
12. Do you get enough drinking water from above?		

13. If no, for how many days it becomes dry?		
14. Do you feel any change in water level in your well after the intervention of watershed in your village, if, yes then what is the change?		

Section – E

Consumption/Expenditure	*2002-03*	*2006-07*
1. How much your family spends on food items in a month? A. Rice B. Ragi C. Dal D. Bajra E. Vegetables F. Other food items		
2. How much your family spends on non-food items in a month/year? A. Cloth B. Fuel C. Medicine D. Education E. Entertainment F. Liquor G. Bidi/Cigarette/Tamakhu H. Festivals		
3. Total Monthly Expenditure		

Section – F

Borrowing	*2002-03*	*2006-07*
1. Do/Did any members of your family borrow money?		
2. What is the loan amount he/she has borrowed? A. .... B. .... C. .... D.		
3. What is the total loan amount of your family?		
4. Did you start repaying the loan amount?		
5. How much have you paid from the total loan amount?		
6. From which source generally you take loan?		
7. What is the rate of interest of the loan you have taken?		
8. Do you keep anything as security to get the loan?		

Section – G

Saving	*2002-03*	*2006-07*
1. Do you/your family member save money?		
2. Generally where do you save money?		
3. What is the total saving amount of your family?		
4. Do you/any one of your family is a member of SHG?		
5. How much do you save in a SHG account?		
6. What is the total value of the SHG account?		
7. Has the SHG received the incentive grant? If yes, what is the amount received?		
8. Has the SHG received any loan from the banks? If so, what is the amount of loan received?		
9. In what way the SHGs utilizes the savings/incentive grants/loan amount?		
10. Is the SHGs are viable now? If yes, in what manner.		

Section – H

Community Participation	*2002-03*	*2006-07*
1. Do you participate in community meetings?		
2. How often do you participate in community meetings?		
3. Are you aware of Immunization, Nutrition, and Hygiene, etc.?		

BASIC INFORMATION OF ________________ MICRO WATERSHED

Name of the Block: ________________ Name of the G.P.: ________________

1. Name of the Watershed : ________________
2. Code No. : ________________
3. Total Geographical Area : ________________
4. Total Treatable Area : ________________
5. Project Outlay : ________________
6. Project Cost per Ha : ________________
7. Project Period : ________________
8. Total Amount Released and Utilized : ________________

Component	*PIA Level*		*Committee Level*		*Total*	
	Allot-ment	*Expen-diture*	*Allot-ment*	*Expen-diture*	*Allot-ment*	*Expen-diture*
Administrative						
Community Organization						
Training						
Works						
Total						

9. Total Area Treated in ha : ________________
10. Demographic Profile:

Sl.No.	*Name of the Village*	*Total Population*	*Male*	*Female*	*SC*	*ST*	*OBC*	*Total*

11. Household Status in the Village:

Sl.No.	*Name of the Village*	*No. of Households in the Watershed*			
		ST	*SC*	*Other Caste*	*Total*

11. Livestock Population:

Type of Livestock	*No.*
1. Cow	
2. Buffalo	
3. Ox	
4. Sheep	
5. Pig	
6. Hen	
7. Duck	
8. Goat	

12. Institutional Arrangements:

(a) Regd. No. of Micro-Watershed Association:

(b) Watershed Level:

Sl.No.	*Designation*	*Name*	*Qualification*	*Caste*
1.	President of Watershed Association			
2.	Chairman of Watershed Committee			
3.	Secretary of Watershed Committee			
4.	Volunteer-I			
5.	Volunteer-II			

(c) P.I.A. Level:

Sl.No.	*Name of the W.D.T. Member*	*Designation*	*Discipline*
1.			
2.			
3.			
4.			
5.			
6.			
7.			

13. Farmers of the Watershed

	Category	No.	
(a)	Small		
(b)	Medium		
(c)	Large		

14. No. of Landless in the Watershed :

15. Literate of the Watershed :

Male	Female	SC	ST	Other	Total

16. Infrastructure :

Sl.No.	Infrastructure	Name and Location
1.	No. of tanks existing in watershed	
2.	Name of the schools	
3.	No. of AWC in the watershed	
4.	No. of community centre	
5.	Whether permanent all weather road to the watershed is available	
6.	Whether P.H.C./Sub-Centre is available	
7.	Whether VD/LAC is available	
8.	No. of wells existing in watershed	
9.	No. of kundi existing in watershed	
10.	Plantation (in ha)	
11.	No. of Grain Banks functioning in the watershed area?	
12.	No. of Joint Forest Management (JFM) Units/ Vana Suraksha Samiti (VSS) functioning in the watershed area?	

17. Capacity Building :

Institution	No.	SC	ST	OC	Total	Women
SHG						
UG						
JFM/VSS						

No. of SHG	Members	Savings	R. Fund	Grade-I	Grade-II	SGSY Linkage

18. W.D.F. Account No. :

19. W.P.A. Account No. :

20. W.D.F. Savings :

21. Major Activities taken up by the SHG:

22. Component-wise details of Expenditure :

(a) Administrative:

Sl.No.	*Name of the Activities*	*Expenditure*
1.	Preparation of Project Report	
2.	Remuneration to the Community Organizer	
3.	Office Stationery for Watershed Committee	
4.	Office Stationery for PIA Office	
5.		
6.		
7.		
8.		
	Total	

(b) Community Organization :

Sl.No.	*Name of the Activities*	*Unit*	*Expenditure*
1.	Participatory Rural Appraisal Exercise		
2.	Wall painting and writing		
3.	Transparency measures		
4.	Health camp		
5.	Animal health camp		
6.	Sprayer machine		
7.	Distribution of vegetable mini kits and high yielding vegetable seeds		
8	Distribution of flower seed		
9.	Distribution of Blanket/Medicated Mosquito net		
10.	Construction of Sadar Mandap		
11.	Construction of tubewell platform		
12.	Celebration of Independence Day		
13.	Celebration of Republic Day		
14.	Celebration of malaria prevention week		
15.	Celebration of water harvesting month		
16.	Celebration of Van Mahotsava		
17.			
18.			
19.			
20.			

(c) Training:

Sl.No.	*Name of the Activities*	*Unit*	*Expenditure*
1.	Training of Watershed functionaries (committee level) at Soil Conservation Training Institute, Koraput for 3 days		
2.	Training to Self-Help Groups on saving mobilization		
3.	Training on women employment		
4.	Training on care of pregnant mother and newly born child to prevent child death rate		
5.	Training on prevention of malaria		
6.	Training on plantation of fruit crops and after care		
7.	Integrated pest management on vegetable crops		
8.	Agricultural training of cultivation of High Yielding Rice		
9.	Off season vegetable cultivation		
10.	Agriculture training on wheat and sunflower cultivation		
11.	Vermi-compost preparation		
12.	Training to U.G. members on contribution and Shramadan		
13.	Training on Pisciculture		
14.	Training on mushroom cultivation to Self-Help Group		
15.	Training on bee-keeping to S.H.G.		
16.	Training on record maintenance of SHG		
17.	Training on record maintenance of watershed committee		
18.	Psicicultural training to Self-Help Group		
19.			
20.			

(d) Works:

Sl.No.	*Item of Work*		*Expenditure*	*Area Treated (in ha)*
1.	Soil and Moisture Conservation			
	(i)			
	(ii)			
	(iii)			
	(iv)			
	(v)			

2.	Water Conservation			
	(i)			
	(ii)			
	(iii)			
	(iv)			
	(v)			
3.	Irrigation			
	(i)			
	(ii)			
	(iii)			
	(iv)			
	(v)			
4.	Plantation/Afforestation			
	(i)			
	(ii)			
	(iii)			
	(iv)			
	(v)			
5.	Livelihood Support			
	(i)			
	(ii)			
	(iii)			
	(iv)			
	(v)			
6.	Others			
	(i)			
	(ii)			
	(iii)			
	(iv)			
	(v)			

23. Complaint

Sl.No.	*Nature of Complaint*	*Action Taken*

24. Difficulties Faced in Course of Undertaking Works .

Sl.No.	*Nature of Difficulty*	*Action Taken*

25. Convergence :

Sl.No.	*Scheme*	*Name of the Work*	*Unit*	*Estd. Cost*

IMPACT ASSESSMENT :

Sl. No.	*Parameter*	*Index of Assessment*	*Before the Project*	*Now*
1.	Area Coverage and Productivity	Increased in cropped area (ha) (a) Kharif (b) Rabi Increased in productivity of two main crops (Qtl/ha) (a) (b)		
2.	Plantation	Position of Trees 1. No. of fruit bearing trees 2. No. of fuelwood trees available		
3.	Livestock	No. of 1. Cattle 2. Sheep 3. Goat 4. Pig 5. Others		
4.	Formation of Groups	No. of SHGs Formed No. of User Group Formed Savings Mobilized		
5.	Contribution	Contribution to W.D.F. (in lakh)		

6.	Education	1. No. of School children in watershed area 2. % of drop-out 3. No. of HSC passed students 4. No. of Intermediate students 5. No. of Graduates 6. No. of Schools in the village		
7.	Income and Expenditure	Average per Capita Income Average per Capita Expenditure		
8.	Migration	No. of migrants 1. Within the State 2. Outside the State		
9.	Liquor	No. of persons with liquor habit		
10.	Sanitation	No. of household having sanitary Latrine No. of household having smokeless chulha No. of household having Bio-gas plant		
11.	Water Sources	No. of Tanks No. of Dug Wells		

BIBLIOGRAPHY

Books

Bagchi, D.K., Maiti, A.K., Sasmal, T.K., Ghosh, T. and Sarkar, K. (1994). "Studies on Micro-Watershed Development in Low Productive Agricultural Systems: Need for an Agro-Ecosystem Approach", *The Challenge of the Balance: Environmental Economics of India*, CSE, New Delhi.

Bardhan, Pranab (1989). "Alternative Approach to the Theory of Institutions in Economic Development", in Bardhan (ed.), *The Economic Theory of Agrarian Institutions*, Clarendon Press, Oxford.

Brooks, K.N., Ffolliot, P.F., Gregersen, H.M. and Debano (1997). *Hydrology and the Management of Watersheds*, Iowa University Press. Ames, Iowa.

Chopra, K. (1999). "Watershed Management Programme: An Evaluation of Alternative Institutional and Technological Options", in *Principles and Practices of Integrated Watershed Management in India*, W/M Publishing, New Delhi.

Chopra, Kanchan, Kadekoli, Gopal and Murthy, M.N. (1990). *Participatory Development: People and Common Property Resources*, Sage Publications, New Delhi.

CSWCRTI (2004). *Participatory Watershed Management for Sustainable Development in Kokriguda Watershed*, Koraput, Odisha under Integrated Wasteland Development Programme, New Delhi. CSWCRTI, Koraput.

Dixon, J. (1977). "Analysis and Management of Watersheds", in P. Dasgupta and K.G. Maler (ed.), *The Environment and Emerging Development Issues*, Vols. I and II, Clarendon Press, Oxford.

Dorfman, Robert and Nancy Dorfman (1977). *Economics of the Environment: Selected Readings*, New York.

Farrington J., Turton, C. and James, A.J. (ed.) (1999). *Participatory Watershed Development: Challenges for 21st Century*, New Delhi.

Foundation for Ecological Security (FES) (2008). *Atlas of Development Trends, District Koraput*, Foundation for Ecological Security.

Glantz, M.H. (1994). *Drought Follows the Plough: Cultivating the Marginal Areas*, Cambridge University Press, Cambridge, U.K.

Government of Odisha (2005). *District Statistical Hand Book*, Koraput.

Government of Odisha (2007). *District Statistical Hand Book*, Koraput.

Government of Odisha (2008). *Statistical Abstract of Odisha*, Directorate of Economics and Statistics, Bhubaneswar.

Government of Odisha (2010). *Economic Survey, 2009-10*, Planning and Coordination Department, Directorate of Economics and Statistics, Government of Odisha.

Government of Odisha (2011). *Economic Survey, 2010-11*, Planning and Coordination Department, Directorate of Economics and Statistics, Government of Odisha.

Honore, Guy (2002). *Principles and Practices of Integrated Watershed Management in India*, IGBP.

Joshi, P.K., Tewari, L., Jha, A.K. and Shiyani, R.L. (2003). *Impact of Watershed Programme and People's Participation*, National Centre for Agricultural Economics and Policy Research (NCAP), New Delhi.

Joy, K.J., Paranjape, S. and Shah, A. (2004). *Scaling Up Watershed Development Projects in India: Learning from First Generation Projects*, Forum for Watershed Research and Policy Dialogue, Bengaluru.

Kollavali, Sashi and John Kerr (2002). "Mainstreaming Participatory Watershed Development", *Economic and Political Weekly*, 1 January, 37(3), pp. 225-42.

Lakshmikanthamma, S. (1997). *Sustainability of Dryland Agriculture in India*, MD Publications, New Delhi.

Maitra, M.K. (2001). *Watershed Management: Project, Planning, Development and Implementation*, Omega Scientific Publishers.

Mani, R. (2006). *Watershed Planning and Employment Generation*, Mittal Publications, New Delhi.

Molden, D. (ed.) (2007). *Water for Food, Water for Life: A Comprehensive Assessment of Water Management in Agriculture*, Earthscan, London.

Pathak, P., Sahrawat, K.L., Rego, T.J. and Wani, S.P. (2005). "Measurable Biophysical Indicators for Impact Assessment: Changes in Soil Quality", in *Natural Resource Management in Agriculture: Methods for Assessing Economic and Environmental Impacts*, CAB International, Wallingford, UK, pp. 53-74.

Pretty and Shah (1996). "Making Soil and Water Conservation Sustainable: From Coercion and Control to Partnership and Participation", in forthcoming *Land Degradation and Rehabilitation*.

Rathod, M.K. (2008). *Tribals and Watershed Development*, Inter India Publications, New Delhi.

Rockstorm, J. (2003). "Water for Food and Nature in Tropics: Vapour Shift in Rainfed Agriculture", Philosophical Transaction of the Royal Society of London Series-B, *Biological Sciences*, 358(1440), 1997-2009.

Rockstorm, J., Hatibu, N., Owesis and Wani, S.P. (2007). "Managing Water in Rainfed Agriculture", in Molden, D. (ed.), *Water for Food and Water for Life: A Comprehensive Assessment of Water Management in Agriculture*, Earthscan, London, U.K and International Water Management Institute, Colombo, Sri Lanka.

Seethapathi, P.V., Dutta, D., Siva Kumar, R. (ed.) (2008). *Hydrology of Small Watersheds*, TERI.

Sharma, Bharat R., Samra, J.S., Scott, C.S. and Wani, S.P. (2005). *Watershed Management Challenges — Improving Productivity, Resources and Livelihood*, International Water Management Institute, Ministry of Agriculture, GoI.

Tideman, E.M. (1996). *Watershed Management: Guidelines for Indian Conditions*, Omega Publishers, New Delhi.

Wani, S.P. (2009). *Rainfed Agriculture: Unlocking the Potential*, CAB International.

Wani, S.P., Pathak, P., Sreedevi, T.K., Singh, H.P. and Singh, P. (2003). "Efficient Management of Rainwater for Increased Crop Productivity and Ground Water Recharge in Asia", in *Water Productivity in Agriculture: Limits and Opportunities for Improvement*, CAB International, Wallingford, U.K. and IWMI, Colombo, Sri Lanka.

Journals

Johnston, D.G. and Mellor, J.W. (1961). "The Role of Agriculture in Economic Development", *American Economic Review*, (51), pp. 566-93.

KRIBHCO (2001). *Watershed Approach for Managing Degraded Lands in India — Challenges for the 21st Century*, KRIBHCO.

Kshirsagar, K.D. and R.D. Ghodake (1991). "Watershed Based Technology: Experience and Lessons", *Indian Journal of Agricultural Economics*, Vol. 46, No. 3, p. 270.

Kumar, Akhilesh and U.K. Saxena, "Moisture Conservation Technique in Dryland Farming", *Indian Farmers Digest*.

Ninan, K.N. (2001). "Poverty and Income Distribution in India", *Economic and Political Weekly*, Vol. 29, pp. 1544-51.

NIRD (1978). *Watershed Management for Resource Development and Conservation in Drought Prone Area*, National Institute of Rural Development, Hyderabad.

Panda, B.K., Panda, R.K. and Sarangi, P. (2006). "Impact of Watershed Development on Dryland Farming in KBK District of Odisha", *Journal of Rural Development*, Volume. 26, No. 2, pp. 189-206, NIRD, Hyderabad.

Rao, C.H.H. (2000). "Watershed Development in India: Recent Experiences and Emerging Issues", *Economic and Political Weekly*, November, 2000

Reddy, V. Ratna (2000). "Sustainable Watershed Management: Institutional Approach", *Economic and Political Weekly*.

Shah, Amita (2002). "Watershed Development Programmes in India — Emerging Issues for Environment Development Perspective", *Economic and Political Weekly*, 33(26): A66-A80.

Soussan, John and V. Ratna Reddy (2003). "Evolving Appropriate Watershed Policy", *Economic and Political Weekly*, 38(1): 24-28.

Sreedevi, T.K., Wani, S.P. and Pathak, P. (2007). "Harnessing Gender Power and Collective Action through Integrated Watershed Management for Minimising Land Degradation and Sustainable Development", *Journal of Financing Agriculture*, 36, 23-32.

Articles

Agarwal, A. (2001). "Common Property Institutions and Sustainable Governance of Resources", *World Development*, 29: 1649-1672.

Agarwal, A. and Narain, S. (1999). *Community and Household Water Management: The Key to Environmental Regeneration and Poverty Alleviation*, Paper presented to EU-UNDP Conference, Brussels.

Agarwal, Bina (2001). "Participatory Exclusions, Community Forestry and Gender: An Analysis for South-Asia and a Conceptual Framework," *World Development*, 29(10): 1623-1648.

Agarwal, A., Narain, S. and Sen, S. (1991). *State of India's Environment: A Citizen's Report — Dying Wisdom*, Centre for Environment, New Delhi.

Anonymous (2005). "Global Food Demand Threatens to Outstrip World Water Supply", *Life Science Weekly*, May 17, World Business Council for Business Development (http:/www.sustainonline.org)

Ashley, Caroline and Diana Carney (1999). *Sustainable Livelihoods: Lessons from Early Experience*, DFID, London.

Awasthi, Ramesh and Dasrath K. Panmand (1994). *Ralegaon Siddhi: A Model for Village Development Foundation for Research in Community Health*, Mumbai.

Bali, J.S. (1988). *A Critical Appraisal of Past and Present Policies and Strategies of Watershed Development and Management in India and Role of Government and Non-governmental Organizations in Small Scale Watershed Development*, Mimeo, SPWD, Workshop.

Butterworth, J., Reddy, M.Y.V. and Batchelor, C. *Addressing Water Needs of the Poor in Watershed Management*, Internet site (http://www.nri.org/WSS_RM/Reports) Last accessed January 2011.

Chopra, Kanchan (1993). "Sustainability of Agriculture", *Indian Journal of Agricultural Economics*, Vol. 48, No. 3, July-September.

Choudhury, P.R. (2005). *Withdrawal Strategy at Micro Watershed Level*, Working Paper No. 50, DFID.

DFID (2002). *Better Livelihoods for Poor People: The Role of Agriculture*, Issue paper, Department of International Development (DFID), London, UK.

Dharia Committee (1995). *Report of the High Level Committee on Wasteland Development*, Government of India, New Delhi.

DRDA, Koraput (2008). *Glimpses of A Milestone Achievement*, District Rural Development Agency, Koraput.

DRDA, Koraput (2005). *SHG Movement in Koraput*, District Rural Development Agency, Koraput.

Falkenmark, M. and Rockstorm, J. (2004). *Balancing Water for Humans and Nature: The New Approach in Ecohydrology*, Earthscan, London, UK.

FAO (2002). *Agriculture: Towards 2015/20*, Technical Interim Report. (http://www.fao.org/es/esd/at2015/toce.htm)

FAOSTAT (2010). http://faostat.fao.org/ (last accessed October, 2010).

Farrington, J. and Crisipino Lobo (1997). *Scaling Up Participatory Watershed Development in India: Lessons from the Indo-German Watershed Development Programme*, ODI Natural Resource Perspectives, No. 17, Overseas Development Institute, London.

Food and Agriculture Organization (FAO) (1987). *Guidelines for Economic Appraisal of Watershed Management Projects*, Conservation Guide No. 16, Rome.

Fujisaka, Sam (1990). *Indigenous Soil and Water Conservation in South-East Asia: Sustainable Agriculture Programme*, Gatekeeper Series, London: IIED.

GoI (1994). *Guidelines for Watershed Development*, Ministry of Rural Development, Government of India.

GoI (1997). *Report on the Committee on Training for Watershed Development*, Eswaran Committee Report, DoLR, MoRD, Government of India, New Delhi.

GoI (2000). *Guidelines for National Watershed Development Projects for Rainfed Area (NWDPRA)*, Rainfed Farming Systems Division, Department of Agriculture and Cooperation, MoA, Government of India, New Delhi.

GoI (2001). *Guidelines for Watershed Development (Revised)*, Department of Land Resources, MoRD, Government of India, New Delhi.

GoI (2008). *Common Guidelines for Watershed Development Projects*, Department of Land Resources, Government of India, New Delhi.

GoI (2009). *Report of the Expert Group to Review the Methodology for Estimation of Poverty*, Planning Commission, Government of India, New Delhi.

GoI (1994). *Report of the Technical Committee on DPAP and DDP*, Ministry of Rural Development, New Delhi.

Government of India (2005). *Serving Farmers and Saving Farming-2006: Year of Agricultural Renewal*, Third Report, 2005. National Commission on Farmers, Ministry of Agriculture, Government of India, New Delhi.

Government of India (2000). *Common Approach for Watershed Development*, New Delhi.

Government of Odisha (1998). *The Path: Watershed Development*, District Rural Development Agency, Koraput.

Government of Odisha (2001). *Watershed Mission*, Odisha Draft Mission Document, Mimeo, Department of Agriculture, Bhubaneswar, Odisha.

Government of Odisha (2002). *Climatological Data of Odisha, 1987-2001*, Directorate of Economics and Statistics, Bhubaneswar, Odisha.

Government of Odisha (1998). *Watershed Management — A Manual*, District Rural Development Agency, Koraput.

Government of Odisha (2001). *User's Manual for Watershed Development*, Watershed Development Mission, Agriculture Department, Government of Odisha, Bhubaneswar.

Government of Odisha (2008). *An Overview of Water Resources of Odisha*, Annual Report, 2008-09, Department of Water Resources, Government of Odisha.

Hinchcliffe, F., Guijt, Irene, Pretty, Jules, N., Shah and Parmesh (2009). *New Horizons: The Economic, Social and Environmental Impacts of Participatory Watershed Development*, Gatekeeper Series No. 50, IIED, Sustainable Agriculture and Rural Livelihoods Programme.

ICRISAT (2006). *ICRISAT's Vision and Strategy to 2015*, ICRISAT, Patencheru, Andhra Pradesh, India.

IFAD (2001). *Rural Poverty Report 2001: The Challenge of Ending Poverty*, International Fund for Agricultural Development, Oxford University Press, Oxford, UK.

IIASA (2002). *Climate Change and Agricultural Vulnerability*, Special Report for the UN World Summit on Sustainable Development, Johannesburg. (http://www.iisa.ac.at/Research/LUC/JB-Report.pdf)

IPCC (2001). *Inter-governmental Panel on Climate Change*, Third Assessment Report, Cambridge University Press, Cambridge, U.K.

Irz, X. and Roe, T. (2000). "Can the World Feed Itself? Some Insight from Growth Theory", *Argekon*, 39(3), 513-528.

Jaitly, A. (2004). "Who Owns Water", *Terragreen*, Vol. I, Issue 1.

Jodha, N.S. (1986). "Common Property Resources and the Rural Poor in Dry Regions of India", *Economic and Political Weekly*, Vol. 54, pp. 1169-1182.

Johnson, N., Ravnborg, H.M., Westerman, O. and Probst, K. (2001). *User Participation in Watershed Management and Research*, Working Paper No. 19, CAPRI, IFPRI, Washington, DC.

Joshi, P.K., Jha, A.K., Wani, S.P., Joshi, L. and Shiyani, R.L. (2005). *Meta Analysis to Assess Impact of Watershed Programme and People's Participation*, Comprehensive Assessment Research Report 8, Comprehensive Assessment Secretariat (IWMI), Colombo, Sri Lanka.

Joshi, P.K., Vasudha Pangare, Shiferaw, B., Wani, S.P., Bouma, J. and Scott, C. (2006). "Socio-economic and Policy Research on Watershed Management in India: Synthesis of the Past Experiences and Needs for Future Research", *An Open Access e-journal* by International Crop Research Institute for Semi-Arid Tropics, Vol. 2, Issue 1.

Kar, Gouranga and Lipi Das (2000). *Sustainable and Effective Watershed Management: A Holistic Approach to Improve Socio-economic Status of Rural Community*.

Kerr, J.M. and Sanghi, N.K. (2002). *Indigenous Soil and Water Conservation in India's Semi-Arid Tropics*, ICRISAT, Hyderabad and National Institute of Agricultural Extension Management (MANAGE), Hyderabad.

Kerr, J.M., Ganesh Pangare, Pangare, V.L. and George, P.J. (2000). *An Evaluation of Dryland Watershed Projects in India*, EPTD

Discussion Paper No. 68, Environment and Production Technology Division, International Food Policy Research Institute, Washington, DC.

Kerr, John and Chung, Kimberly (2001). *Evaluating Watershed Management Projects*, CAPRI Working Paper No. 17.

Kerr, John (2002). "Watershed Development: Environmental Services and Poverty Alleviation in India", *World Development*, 1387-1400.

Kerr, J., Pangare, G. and Pangare, V.L. (2002). *Watershed Development Projects in India: An Evaluation*, International Food Policy Research Institute (IFPRI), New Delhi.

Kerr, J.M., Sanghi, N.K. and Sriramappa, G. (1996). "Subsidies in Watershed Development Projects in India: Distortions and Opportunities", *IIED Gatekeeper Series 61*, London: International Institute for Environment and Development.

Kumar, Kundan, Kerr, John and Choudhury, P.R. *Tenure and Access Rights as Constraints to Watershed Development in Odisha*, India.

Ministry of Rural Development (1994). *Guidelines for Watershed Development*, Ministry of Rural Development, Government of India.

Mishra, B. *A Successful Case of Participatory Watershed Management at Ralegaon Siddhi Village, District Ahmednagar, Maharashtra*, AVARD, New Delhi.

Odisha Tribal Empowerment and Livelihood Project (OTELP) (2007). *Assessment Survey for Designing Comprehensive Livelihoods Strategy*, Study Conducted by KCSD, Bhubaneswar, Knowledge Trust, Bhubaneswar and NRMC, New Delhi.

Panda, D.K. (2003). *Economics of Watershed Treatment — A Case Study in Odisha*.

Pangare, Vasudha L. (1998). *Gender Issues in Watershed Development and Management in India*, Agricultural Research and Extension Network Paper 88, ODI, London, UK.

Pathak, P., Wani, S.P. and Sudi, R. (2006). *Gully Control in SAT Watersheds*, Global Theme on Agro Ecosystems Report No. 15, ICRISAT, Patencheru, Andhra Pradesh.

Planning Commission (1973). *Report on Task Force on Integrated Rural Development in Drought Prone Areas*, Government of India, New Delhi.

Rajesekhar, D., Gopalappa, D.V. and Madhushree Sekhar (2003). *Role of Local Organizations in Watershed Development*, Project Report, Institute for Social and Economic Change, Bengaluru.

Sahu, S.K. (2005). *Cost Benefit Analysis of Watershed Management: A Comparative Study of Selected Projects in Odisha and Rajasthan*.

Samal, Jagabandhu (2011). *Economic Empowerment of Tribals through SHG*, Presented in National Seminar on Challenges in Preservation and Development of Tribal Culture.

Samra, J.S. (2000). *Assessment of Participatory Process of Watershed Management.*

Samuel, Abrahm, Joy, K.J., Suhas Paranjape, Eshwer Kale, Raju Adgale and Ravi Pomane (2005). *Watershed Development in Maharashtra: A Large Scale Rapid Assessment*, SOPPECOM, Forum for Watershed Research and Policy Dialogue.

Seth, S.L. and Soren Damgaard-Larsen (2002). *Participatory Watershed Development Approach*, DANIDA's Watershed Programme.

Sharma, Rita (2001). *Development of Land for Sustainable Agricultural Production*, Ministry of Agriculture, Government of India, New Delhi.

Singh, Kartar (1995). *The Watershed Management Approach to Sustainability of Renewable Common Pool Natural Resources: Lessons from India's Experience*, Research Paper No. 14, Institute of Rural Development, Anand.

Sreedevi, T.K., Shiferaw, B. and Wani, S.P. (2004). *Adarsha Watershed in Kothapally: Understanding the Drivers of Higher Impact*, Global Theme on Agro-ecosystems, Report No. 10 (ICRISAT), Patencheru, Andhra Pradesh.

Sreedevi, T.K., Wani, S.P., Sudi, R., Mahesh, S., Patel, J.T., Singh, S.N. and Shah, T. (2006). *On-site and Off-site Impact of Watershed Development: A Case Study of Rajasamadhiyala, Gujarat*, Global Theme on Agro-ecosystem, Report No. 20, ICRISAT, Patencheru.

Thirtle, C., Beyers, Lin, L., Mckenzie-Hill, V., Irz, X., Wiggins, S. and Pisse, J. (2002). *The Impacts of Changes in Agricultural Productivity on Incidence of Poverty in Developing Countries*, DFID Report No. 7946, DFID, London, U.K.

Turton, C., Coulter, J., Shah, A. and Farrington, J. (2003). *Watershed Development in India: Impact of 1994 Guidelines*, A report prepared for Government of India and DFID, New Delhi, 1998.

UN Millennium Project (2005). *Investing in Development: A Practical Plan to Achieve the Millennium Development Goals*, UN MDG, New York (www.unmilleniumproject.org).

UNSTAT (2009). www.unstat.org last accessed 2010.

Vaidyanathan, A. (1991). *Integrated Watershed Development: Some Major Issues*, Foundation Day Lecture, Society for Promotion of Watershed Development, New Delhi.

Van Koppen, B., Namara, R. and Stafilios-Rostchild, C. (2005). *Reducing Poverty through Investment in Agricultural Water Management*, Poverty and Gender issues and synthesis of sub-Saharan Africa Case Study Reports, Working Paper 101, International Water Management Institute (IWMI), Colombo, Sri Lanka.

Wani, S.P., Ramakrishna, Y.S., Sreedevi, T.K., Long, T.D., Wangkahart, T., Shiferaw, B., Pathak, P. and Kesava Rao, A.V.R. (2006). *Issues, Concepts, Approaches and Practices in Integrated Watershed Management: Experience and Lessons from Asia*, Proceedings of the International Workshop held at ICRISAT, Nairobi.

WASSAN (2001). *Issues Relating to Dalits, Livelihoods, and Watershed*, Watershed Support Services and Activities Network, Secunderabad.

WHO (2000). *Gender, Health and Poverty*, Fact Sheet No. 25, (http://www.who.int/mediacentre/factsheets)

World Bank (2005). *Agricultural Growth for the Poor: An Agenda for Development*, The International Bank for Reconstruction and Development/The World Bank, Washinton DC.

World Bank (2008). *World Development Report*, Oxford University Press, U.K.

World Bank (1991). *Policy Isssues and World Bank Experience in Multipurpose River Basin Development*, The World Bank, Washington DC.

World Bank (2006). *Managing Watershed Externalities in India*, Agriculture and Rural Development Sector Unit, Discussion Paper Series, Report No. 1.

INDEX